# The Political Economy of New India

## Critical Essays

# The Political Economy of New India

## Critical Essays

Raju J Das

AAKAR

*The Political Economy of New India: Critical Essays*
Raju J Das



First Published 2020
Reprinted 2021
**Reprinted 2026**

ISBN 978-93-5002-634-2



**AAKAR BOOKS**
28 E Pocket IV, Mayur Vihar Phase I
Delhi 110 091, India
www.aakarbooks.com

*Designed by*
Limited Colors, Delhi

*Printed at*
D.K. Fine Art Press, Delhi

*[The wealthy] … will have to protect themselves from the resentment of the poor and will live in fear more and more, as is already the case in a number of countries. Any society where the rich are too rich and the poor too poor will generate violence, crime and civil war. Agitators can easily get the poor to rise up [against the rich]…'*

[Dalai Lama (2001) *Daily advice from the heart*]

***

*As long as the shackles of wealth and property bind us, we will remain accursed forever and never attain the altar of humanity, which is life's ultimate goal.*

[Premchand (1958) *Godaan*]

***

*Where the mind is without fear and the head is held high*
*Where knowledge is free*
*Where the world has not been broken up into fragments*
*By narrow domestic walls*
*Where words come out from the depth of truth*
*Where tireless striving stretches its arms towards perfection*
*Where the clear stream of reason has not lost its way*
*Into the dreary desert sand of dead habit*
*Where the mind is led forward by thee*
*Into ever-widening thought and action*
*Into that heaven of freedom, my Father, let my country awake.*

[Rabindranath Tagore (1910) *Gitanjali*]

*This book is dedicated to the millions of workers and small-scale producers of multiple religions and castes in India. They live and work in a system that is dominated by a tiny profit-seeking class of large property-owners, a class that is well supported by a political, bureaucratic and intellectual elite. These millions of men, women and children are unable to meet their very basic needs and are increasingly being deprived of their democratic rights. Yet, it is only they who can change their conditions through their own democratically-organized struggles at multiple geographical scales and in multiple spheres of life.*

# Contents

# 1
# Introduction

India has been undergoing momentous changes in the economic and political spheres of life. Those who control India's resources and political institutions are engaged in actions that adversely affect the country's majority, i.e. the workers and small-scale producers, including peasants. While there has been a Right-ward turn, the Left appears to be increasingly weak. These changes occurring in Indian society are the focus of this book. The economic and political elites know extremely well what they are doing. They, more or less, control the production and dissemination of ideas, including through the media and the academic world, that inform their actions and promote their interests. But do the masses—or at least, the educated elements among the masses—also have a similar level of knowledge about what is being done to them and what is to be done to change their situation?

Much intellectual writing is either too much based in raw facts (which are often in the form of statistical information about what is happening), so it fails to give an explanatory interpretation of the big picture, or it is based on convoluted conceptual arguments, often with numerous citations and with statements about who said what, with little clear linkage to the real world. Besides, much intellectual work is inadequately critical of social-economic power relations in society or it is not critical at all. More specifically, it fails to adequately situate the changes happening in society in their proper class context, i.e. the context that is defined by the interests and ideas of the economic elite, supported by those who manage the state and by those who control ideas and actions in 'civil society' (the sphere that is outside the economy and the state). The absence of critical thinking, a hallmark of which is the erasure of distinctions in society that is based on class (and social oppression) is especially noted since a pro-market, pro-business turn occurred in the sphere of economic and social policy, since the late 1980s. This is a turn that seeks to obviate, and indeed delegitimize, critical thinking in the name of what is called development or, worse, national development, or national interest, and in the name of good governance. This lack of critical attitude is, more or less, a worldwide trend.

It is also the case that: whether a piece of writing is empirical or conceptual, it is not presented from the standpoint of ordinary educated men and women. That is, it is not always presented in the form in which an educated, intelligent person without a specialist knowledge of a subject can understand the crux of the argument. All this is true about much intellectual writing in general. This is true about intellectual writings about India.[1]

There is absolutely a role for academic writing and research for a specialist audience. I have written this kind of material myself, more recently a book on the nature of the social critique itself and on the various ways in which critique can be produced (Das, 2014) or indeed how to theorize class inequality and to critically examine society from a consistently class-based perspective (Das, 2017a; Das, 2020). Like other academic writers, I have enjoyed doing so. However, those in academia have a public role: to disseminate difficult ideas in a simple manner so that both academics as well as educated people outside of academia can understand, in order to make sense of what is happening around them and to act on what is happening, if necessary/possible.

It is from this standpoint that this relatively short book is written. This book represents a contradiction. On the one hand, I do believe that research on society must be difficult (Das, 2012a). It must be difficult in part because what appears to be the case is not indeed the case, so one has to go beneath the surface appearances. To be able to do that requires theorization, and theorization, which involves abstraction,[1] among many other things, is hard labour (Das, 2012b; Sayer, 1992). On the other hand, research should not be entirely for researchers. Researchers are able to do research partly because they receive support from ordinary people.[3] Therefore, this book is partly a response to the advice I have received from colleagues and students and to my own realization that I write for the working masses (and younger scholars who have just begun their serious study).[4]

The book is conceptually driven and is a result of research, but it seeks to avoid the 'perils' of academicism.[5] The essays that make up the book provide short and critical commentaries on different aspects of Indian economy or polity or where these spheres meet. The book discusses some of the themes that are being constantly talked about and are of relevance to ordinary people in India: agrarian crisis; farmers' suicides; neoliberal economic policy; protests against dispossession; poverty; the state of democracy; and the religious Right, etc.

The discussion in this book aims to help us to see society in India (and elsewhere), in terms of the reciprocal interaction between the economic and the political processes, and in terms of unequal power relations (between the rich and the poor, and between state elites and ordinary citizens) that determine the nature of that interaction. This is a standpoint that allows one to envisage a future society that is deeply democratic in all spheres of human society. The nature of the discussion presented here is informed by, and is hoped to shed light on, the fact that ordinary people's right to live a decent life has not been quite respected, and that, in more recent times, there has been an attack on India's democratic and secular tradition.[6]

As mentioned, the book seeks to promote a critical imagination among the educated strata of the working people, including, but not just, those who are in the universities and colleges, so the degree of academic nature of the discussion, with its usual protocols (references, quotations, detailed presentations of various sides of a debate, etc.), is kept to the minimum, although some Chapters are somewhat more academic in nature than others. The book talks about what has been happening in just one country, India, which is, arguably, a most interesting labouratory for social science research, given its combined and uneven development.[7] It is hoped that people living in other parts of South Asia, and indeed in the global south, can relate to its content.

There are 12 Chapters in the remainder of the book. Chapter 2 talks about the nature of neoliberalism (i.e. neoliberal capitalist class relations), and the state of the Indian economy in the aftermath of the 2008 global economic crisis. Chapter 3 reflects on a specific issue that is, in many ways, a manifestation of neoliberal capitalism: the continuing agrarian crisis and farmers' suicides. This topic is examined from a theoretical standpoint that places the Indian economy in its global context, arguing that the agrarian crisis is not merely agrarian.

A major tendency of neoliberal capitalism is towards the commodification of everything. This includes education. Chapters 4-5 shed light on the commodification of one aspect of education, i.e. preparation for entrance exams for civil services and for professional—especially technical—education. These Chapters reflect on the nature of the craze for civil services and for technical education, and on how this is connected to the class character of the Indian economy and polity.

With the onset of neoliberalism there has also risen a right-wing view of economic development (and of society and polity, in general). Chapters 6-7 offer a critical reflection on what is being called the Gujarat model of development or 'Modani' model of development, and on the Hindu Right's world-view, including its view of nationalism. Among other things what this discussion suggests is that: as long as there are conditions in the world which make people follow a religion, they should have the freedom to do so, that all religions contain, however contradictorily and inadequately, some humanistic and lofty ideas about humanity (while they also contain regressive ideas and promote political passivity), that no religious group (the majority or a minority) should suffer from discrimination, that no religion should be seen as inferior or superior to another, that affairs of the state and politics should be kept away from people's religious views/practices (to the maximum extent possible), and that no one should be allowed to politicize people's religiosity and mobilize public support, covertly or overtly, in the name of religion. The Chapters also argue that society's problems such as poverty, unemployment, low wages, etc. do not fundamentally exist because of the religious divide but that when religion-based politics and policies in support of neoliberal capitalism are combined and reinforce each other, problems get worse and economic development gets more lopsided, that the politically-manufactured conflict between religions diverts attention from the real cause of society's problems that affect the common people of all religions, which points to the need to unite them across the religious divide, to demand democratic and social rights, etc.

Chapters 8-9 broaden the scale of analysis to consider the problem of poverty as such. Proverbially associated with India, poverty has to be seen in terms of the class character of society—i.e. in terms of the question of who controls society's resources and whether they are used for profit or to meet people's needs. After introducing briefly, what a class analysis of poverty might look like, Chapter 8 critically reflects on the weakness of the Left's theory of Indian society, partly in relation to the problem of poverty. The next Chapter discusses in some detail the connection between the state and poverty, arguing that the capitalist state is a main cause—if not the main cause—of the continued existence of poverty in a class-divided society such as India's.

Chapters 10-13 turn to progressive-politics-from-below. Chapter 10 discusses the crisis of development as the crisis of livelihood and provides critical reflections on the politics of protest against neoliberalism. The idea of protests against neoliberalism, including against SEZs, is found to be inadequate. If that is the case, and if the right-wing politics (discussed in

Chapters 8-9) is also problematic, then the question is: what is to be done?

This matter is discussed in Chapters 11-13, from the standpoint of the economic, social and political rights of the workers and small-scale producers, who are the majority of the nation, but from a perspective that is also critical of the current theory and practice of the Left. These three Chapters constitute the conclusion part of the book. Together they argue for a stronger Left that must work on the basis of united front principles to become a tribune of the people, to fight against tyranny and oppression wherever they exist. The Left should promote a counter-hegemonic class-consciousness of the masses through a critical engagement with theoretical ideas that explain the nature of capitalist society and the nature of a relatively less developed capitalist society such as India's.[8] This is a consciousness that imagines a new society, one that is thoroughly democratic in every sphere of life (economic, political, etc.), and that is based on the principle that society's resources should be collectively controlled by, and in the interest of, ordinary men, women and children (i.e. those who perform the bulk of the skilled and unskilled work, some of whom may be slightly better off than others) to meet their material and cultural needs. Such a society is very different from the current Indian society where one per cent of the population controls more than half of its wealth, and which decides the economic and political conditions, and where the vast majority of the people are unemployed or under-employed, or when employed, they are not earning an income to allow them to experience a decent standard of living. A counter-hegemonic consciousness must seek to undermine any existing hegemonic consciousness from the side of the Right or the Centre, that often seeks to support/justify one or both of the following in varying degrees:

(a) an attack on democratic rights of people to freely express one's ideas and to engage in acts of resistance that do not resort to unprovoked violence, an attack that is increasingly manifested in communal terms (i.e. attack on religious minorities) and casteist terms (i.e. attack on Dalits); and

(b) a system of class-exploitation, as well as dispossession of small-scale producers, and privatization of public resources (e.g. state-owned companies; government-owned land or forests) in order to increase profits in the hands of domestic and foreign businesses.

A counter-hegemonic consciousness must also seek to be critical of the existing hegemonic consciousness from the Left. This has taken at least two forms. One is that while in power, the Left has practised neoliberal policies. But more importantly, the Left's general vision is to confine itself, more or less, to a fight for a modification of the current system to make it slightly more tolerable, including on the basis of trade union struggles and putting pressure on the state for minimally pro-poor and easily reversible policies, without such a fight being conducted within the framework of the fight to transcend the system itself in order to establish democracy in every sphere of life which would allow the common people, those who perform manual and mental labour for a wage/salary, to control the use of society's resources to satisfy their need.[9]

I understand that the views expressed in the book, including about what is to be done by the Left, may be considered unfashionable in the current times. So let me conclude this introduction with a short poem I wrote a few years ago.

A street vendor of antiques am I
A seller of things people adored in 'olden' times
I like what I offer for 'sale'
Which I want others to just try
If people passing by do not want my things,
they go their way, and I go mine,
to set up my shop in places new,
always wishing a day will come when
someone will say 'I like what you like'
and whisper in my ears 'I am with you'.

## Notes

1. This is only a broad generalization. It is to be stressed that numerous critical writings for the educated public do appear in national newspapers and magazines (e.g. *The Hindu, The Statesman, Frontline, Outlook, Mainstream, Seminar, Economic and Political Weekly*, etc.) and online (e.g. *Sanhati, Radical Notes, Macroscan*, etc.). Consider also such books as Utsa Patnaik's highly readable *Republic of Hunger* or Nayyar and Bhaduri's *The Intelligent Person's Guide to Liberalization* or Thapar et al's *Nationalism.*
2. Things in the world are interconnected which means that what one thing is it is because of its relations with other things, so one has to abstract from certain things to be able to shed light on other things, and that requires one to be able to intelligently draw boundaries around the topics/processes of interest to the researcher at a given point in time. Deciding what to include under the scope of a given concept and what not to, is not an easy task to do, and given that without concepts one cannot properly understand what is happening around us, being able to engage in abstraction is crucial to the task of understanding the world. There are several methods of abstraction (for a discussion on this, and how they can be applied to the study of society, see Das, 2017a: Chapter 5; Ollman, 2003).
3. There are several relevant aspects here. 1. To do research, researchers must satisfy their needs. Indeed, people first of all satisfy their need for food, clothing and shelter (*roti, kapda* and *makaan*), before they can take part in politics or paint or study. In the wider social division of labour, researchers do not produce the things they need in order to survive (e.g. food, shelter, etc.) because the work of material production is done by others (including their parents and other family members) who do not have the time to spend as much time as the specialists do, thinking about society. 2. The direct and indirect taxes that ordinary people pay support academic work. 3. Researchers gain knowledge about society by interacting with ordinary people.
4. When I was invited to give a talk at Utkal University, Bhubaneswar, at an academic event where there were professors, students and activists, Mr. Sudhir Patnaik, the eminent progressive journalist from Odisha, during his kind remarks on my talk, stressed the need to write for an educated, non-academic audience.
5. There are many perils of academicism which result in the fact that research is often only for the sake of researchers. These perils include: expressing a simple idea in a difficult and convoluted way so that what one says appears to be more erudite than it actually is; cluttering written lines with numerous references to other people's work for the above-mentioned purpose; using 'on the one hand and on the other hand' type argument, thus avoiding a clear stance, where it is not necessary

to do so; and, going on and on about who said what, instead of saying what one wants to say or what the crux of the matter is.

6. It should be noted that the book generally does not touch on the post-2014 regime under the BJP, but it does deal with some of the processes that were already evident before the 2014 general election.
7. This is the idea that not only do different areas develop unequally under market relations but also is it the case that modern market relations based on the principle of equal and un-coerced exchange are superimposed on—combined with—archaic relations (of unfreedom).
8. It is suggested that people should engage, with a curious and critical attitude, with Marxist texts, including Marx's *Capital*, even if one may not agree with everything that these texts say.
9. It is the last type of consciousness that most segments of the Left currently promote.

# 2
# Neoliberal India and Indian Economy-in-Crisis, Post 2008*

The elite in India and the Western world incessantly blathers about India's 'rise'. Two points must be made straightway about this. First, the so-called rise of India is really the rise of big business (domestic and foreign) and more privileged layers of the mainly city-based middle class,[1] who are most connected to the big business groups. India's so-called rise and its high growth rate have happened mainly through the super-exploitation of its skilled and unskilled workers, dispossession of small-scale-producers, and, a massive ecological devastation.[2]

Second, and in spite of all these methods of exploitation and transfer of resources to the business class, the story of India's rise lost much of its pre-2008 shine in the aftermath of the crisis: the combined effect of the global economic crisis and India's own political-economic problems has contributed to the dampening of India Inc's ambitions to further transform the country into a low-wage platform of global capitalism (and into a subordinate 'partner' of Western imperialism vis-a-vis its major competitor in the south, i.e. China, with which it also has geopolitical tensions). All this is being registered in the press. England's *Economist* ran a cover-story titled 'India's economy losing its magic. Reverberations of India's crisis are heard even in Canada (whose companies including Bombardier have

* This Chapter does not talk about the economic situation during the current BJP rule.

much stake in India): a *Toronto Star* article said: 'After years of basking in praise—"the second biggest economy in Asia," an "emerging power," and "an economic powerhouse"—India has hit a rough patch' (Dhillon, 2011).

The big business and the political elite in India, like elsewhere in the world, responded to the global economic crisis, in part by pressing for an acceleration of pro-market reforms, including the gutting of remaining restrictions on layoffs and enterprise closures, and cuts to the meagre subsidies and social sector spending. This is a process that represents an intensification of the ongoing assault on the living standards of the working people. By reducing domestic demand, such an assault is partly behind the stalling of the growth process itself. India's story suggests this simple principle: in a globalized economy dominated by financial (and imperialistic) capital, there are strong limits to what businesses and governments can achieve within a country, in terms of productive investment and in terms of promoting economic development that is sustainable in a social-ecological sense and that is in the interest of the people who produce wealth. This is especially true in a less developed country such as India with extremely low levels of per-hour labour productivity, a massive reserve army of under- and unemployed people (including millions of inter-regional and rural-urban migrants), and enormous absolute poverty, and whose position in the global capitalist economy is one of a low-wage platform which must produce things/services for imperialist centres at a low cost.

## India's Neoliberalism[3]

In 1991 India had to obtain emergency IMF support and abandon state-led national-capitalist economic growth in favour of full integration into the world capitalist market. It launched a new economic policy (NEP) or "economic reforms"—a euphemism for welfare spending cuts and concessions/incentives for the business class (the moneybags) and lifting of regulations on this class. NEP expresses specific demands to create conditions where domestic and foreign capital can invest money to make a lot of money and do so quickly, by using India's natural resources (e.g. land, water, minerals and forests) that are made available at a cheap rate, and relatively cheap skilled and unskilled labour, and via speculation and other non-productive means. All existing barriers to capitalist accumulation—and these include state-owned enterprises, the existence of which has till recently restricted what private enterprises can produce for a profit—should be removed. Specific economic demands of the business class[4] are politically expressed as NEP, which is pursued by various governments installed at provincial and federal levels include: deregulation of private business; privatization of government-owned businesses; trade liberalization; allowing entry of foreign capital to own business in India; tax cuts for big business; provision of under-valued assets and other incentives for business; making it possible to easily acquire land and other resources owned by small-scale producers; and withdrawal or reduction of meagre government benefits for the poor. The NEP therefore is the neo-liberal programme of the bourgeoisie first, and a government's policy second.[5]

NEP has produced, at least during the 2003-08 period, a high growth rate (8-9 per cent). There was an increase in investment: percentage of gross domestic capital formation to GDP increased, first slowly from the early 1990s, then relatively at a faster rate since early 2001. This process pushed up aggregate demand which led to an increase in production and income which in turn fed back into increased production.[6] Much of the growth process was based on the state bribing the business class, i.e. giving away natural resources at cheap rates and on elite consumption (and investment demand), driven by debt-financing (bank credit). The latter was in turn possible due to inflows of foreign capital, including from the US, which had a low interest rate, searching for quick profits overseas.[7] These inflows have been important to sustain an economy such as that of India in which and unlike in China, investment outstrips savings. On the international front as well, since 2001 at least, imports have outstripped exports, producing trade deficits, which grew fastest, especially during the years of highest growth (2003-08). One reason is that the affluent section of the population buys a lot of imported items, as final goods or as intermediate goods. Given the nature of growth, those sectors which produce for the rich, grew much faster than other sectors (e.g. food production).

The growth process has been deeply un-equalizing (Kohli, 2012). It has led to a small minority of winners and a very large majority of losers, solidly dividing the country into two vastly unequal parts (roughly the top 20 per cent and bottom 80 per cent). It has vastly benefited the capitalist class, including its financial elements, producing more than 100 dollar- billionaires. According to a widely circulated Credit Suisse report: in India, in 2015, the richest 1 per cent own 53 per cent of the country's wealth, and the share of the top 10 per cent of the population is 76.3 per cent of the country's wealth (Chakravarty, 2016).[8] It has placed a colossal amount of wealth in the hands of a few, the wealth produced by the sweat of the masses, who have practically no property. A part of the new wealth created that has gone to the super-wealthy has been hidden away in overseas banks, and another part is publicly displayed via pretentious lifestyles.[9] A wide variety of consumer items, including from the rich countries, is now available for those with money (approximately 200 millions in the country of 1200 millions). It has also benefited some educated people—including tech-coolies—employed in IT and related industries providing cheap skilled labour to global capitalism. The economic success of this stratum is mobilized as an ideological prop for NEP. Elements of this strata, including those with technical and scientific education, have also been a support base for socially conservative obscurantist, irrational ideas, and attendant reactionary politics of hyper religious nationalism.

On the other hand: NEP has heaped unspeakable agony, miseries and degradation on the other pole (the bottom 800 or so millions): the proletarians and semi-proletarians (the people who mainly/entirely depend on wages) and vast numbers of small-scale business/land owners and self-employed people.

NEP has produced a massive amount of economic inequality, economic insecurity, unemployment and under-employment, casualization, contractorization, informalization, speed-up, heightened level of labour exploitation, and lax or non-implementation of protective factory acts. It has produced a graveyard of people who are committing suicides (one farmer kills himself/herself every half an hour), because they cannot pay their bills. Economically insecure people are committing suicide not just in villages, but also in erstwhile booming cities such as Tirupur where labourers kill themselves. At least one-fifth of India's total population is undernourished. The government-mandated minimum wages are below what a working class family needs to live a decent life. While a family of three needs no less than Rs. 20,000 a month or Rs. 600 a day, the average wages are barely Rs. 300 a day.

The extent of class inequality can be made sense of from the Figure below on organized manufacturing: the ratio of profits to net value added or output has been rising since the 1990s while wages as a ratio of value added has been falling in spite of an increase in productivity per worker.

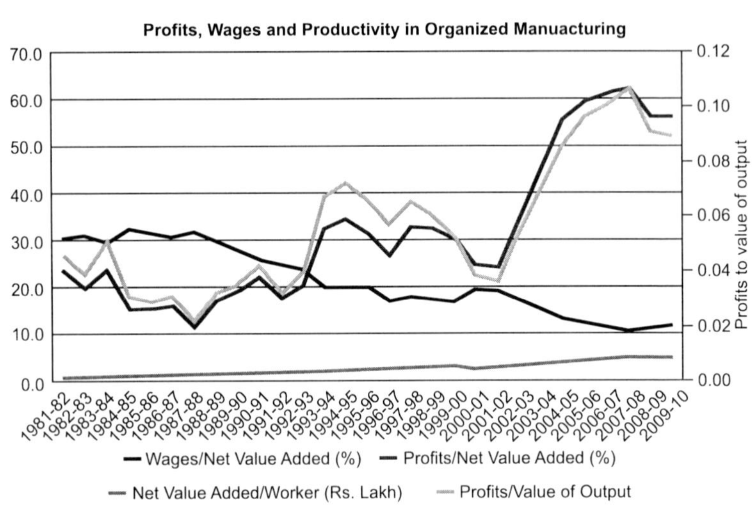


Figure 1: Profit, Wages and Productivity in Manufacturing in India's Organized Sector

*Source:* Chandrasekhar and Ghosh, 2012

What is to be further noted is that: of the components of the net value added, the nominal value of wages rose only marginally, but the increase in profits and in emoluments, which include managerial salaries, was substantial. The increase in non-wage salaries and incomes not only directly drives manufacturing demand, but also provides the basis for the expansion of credit-financed investment and consumption expenditure. Thus the boom creates conditions that also help prolong that boom (Chandrasekhar and Ghosh, 2012).

On the one hand, rural areas have become an arena of capitalist accumulation in newer ways: buying peasants' land at a dirt cheap price; contract farming; cultivation of capital-intensive high-value farm products such as flowers and shrimps in a country (where millions even do not have access to rice or wheat or a glass of safe water to drink); agribusiness sale of farm inputs such as seeds to peasants; and patenting of indigenous knowledge of peasants. On the other hand, rural areas have been subjected to state neglect partly in order to make resources available for investment in infrastructure for big business to slash taxes on big business: rural development expenditure as a percentage of the net national product has been decreasing.[10] Government subsidies for fertilizers, healthcare, electricity and other farm inputs and investment in irrigation have been slashed. Access to cheap loans to farmers has been limited. Price supports to farmers have been reduced, and the Public Distribution System has been drastically curtailed. The so-called rural employment guarantee programme aims to provide minimum wage work for a hundred days to a family member, but it is too little help. It is also not receiving adequate financial support.

Peasants are losing land to capitalist industrialization and land-speculation. Land ceilings laws are reversed because these are considered to be constraints on capital flows into farming. Peasants are being forced to leave their land because farming is not viable: costs of cultivation are rising due to shrinking government support. Highly indebted, many are driven to distress sales of their product. They are also affected by the import of subsidized foreign farm goods.

As Professor Utsa Patnaik (2007) has admirably documented, food production and availability per capita is decreasing, in part because land is converted to non-food crops both by big companies and smaller owners attracted by the prospect of making a little cash. This is a grave danger to food security. Also, in the areas where high-value farm products are produced (shrimps; flowers), an intense exploitation of labour and land happens in order to make the sector competitive in the global market (Das, 2014b). Declining investment in rural infrastructure (especially flood and irrigation control) is increasing vulnerability to drought and floods. Agrarian distress is creating a huge reserve army, a part of which is forced to migrate to cities, putting pressure on wages which are already very low. This, along with shrinking government support for workers, allows capital to raise the level of exploitation.

In other words, what is happening is this. In rural areas, NEP is driven by an internally contradictory logic: enhancing the value of rural areas as an arena for big business activities; and reducing state investment in rural areas, whether for promoting rural economic development or social welfare, in order to make available funds for building infrastructure dominantly for use by big business.

On its own terms, NEP is not a great success either. It has indeed unleashed the animal spirits and created a new generation of investors. Yet, India still accounts for barely 2 per cent of the global economy and 1 per cent of world trade. Even in the IT sector, India remains a relatively minor player dependent on the technology and markets of the West. There is hardly any sign that in key sectors, the average level of labour productivity per hour (not per worker) has improved relative to that in richer countries. India remains a cheap labour platform of global capitalism.

Development often means construction of the physical infrastructure (bijli, sadak and pani) in both politicians' speeches and in the popular discourse. Ideally, the masses can benefit from development-as-infrastructure: who does not need good roads or electricity? But in a market-driven profit-oriented system, things that people need are not just things. They become commodities: things that are bought and sold for a profit. Then the problem becomes this: while people need things such as *bijli, sadak, pani*, etc., they do not have the monetary means to purchase access to these.[11] On the other hand, the production of these commodities becomes a means of making an enormous amount of money, both for the business class, and for the politicians/officials who are involved in the 'regulation' of such construction.

NEP has also resulted in an enormous amount of unevenness between regions, because neoliberal investment, whose main motive is profit-making, tends to be geographically concentrated, although the patterns of unevenness may change over time. The places which are attractive to businesses may not be the places where new investment is most needed from the standpoint of satisfying people's needs. Investment goes to those places where profit can be made (i.e. where physical and social infrastructures already exist), and often, businesses look for above-average profit, and not just profit. Investment does happen in a few places or states, producing impressive glass buildings, gorgeous shopping malls and islands of 'hi-tech' firms, but this does not mean that all the places in the country can experience this. A most important form of this unevenness is between rural and urban areas. Urban areas grow 500 per cent times faster than rural areas. Agriculture has, more or less, stagnated partly because public expenditure, as mentioned earlier, has dwindled, and public resources are diverted from it to infrastructure projects that mainly serve the interest of big business. The geographical face of the country outside cities and their closely connected hinterlands is dismal; this is not to deny enormous unevenness between the richer areas inside cities (e.g. gated communities vs slums) or that a tiny elite in rural areas, and especially in villages close to big cities and newly industrializing places, have benefited by supplying things to the city-based businesses. One of the best indicators of development is infant mortality: rural-urban differences in infant mortality are enormous. It is: 54.7 per thousand of live births in rural areas and 34.7 in urban areas in 2008 (Mukunthan, 2015).

The patterns of uneven development have an interesting political dynamics, between cities and states. With pro-business reforms, regional political elites, who represent regional (provincial) and city-based enterprise-owners and land-owners, have more power now vis-a-vis the central government, and these regionally-based elites compete with each other for external loans and domestic as well as foreign capital. Some states (and some cities) get more investment than others, thus creating a new layer of uneven economic development. When all places are equally neoliberal in courting capital, small differences in policy or other factors necessary for profitmaking become metamorphosed into large differences.

Natural resources, markets, space (including spaces to dump wastes and refuel military planes) and cheap labour of poorer countries cannot be entirely left in the hands of the national bourgeoisie to exploit. International capital and its powerful national states must have free access to these. NEP, which is the medium of, and outcome of, global neoliberalism, playing itself out in India, establishes a direct exploitative connection between the bourgeoisie of rich countries and India's poor masses to a degree that did not exist earlier. Such transfer of resources occurs via exploitation of workers, and exploitation and dispossession of peasants of India (as of other peripheral-capitalist countries) by imperialist capital, and abuse of the environment, a process that NEP furthers. This imperialist exploitation is abetted by the states of imperialist countries and India's pliant-'compradore' state, which is epitomized in sultans of economic reforms (read: pro-business policies hurting ordinary citizens).[12] These sultans, the reforms-mongers, are equally present in all major parties, whether Congress or BJP; it is in fact not an exaggeration to say that BJP is a Right version of Congress (to the extent that any differences in economic policy do exist), and mainstream Left parties are, in practice, generally a mildly Left version of Congress. It is also interesting that some of the Indian states are run under budgetary guidelines formulated by the US 'knowledge' firm McKinsey, the IMF and the World Bank and DFID and 'compradore' intellectuals and advisors 'bought off' by these institutions. In many ways, neoliberalism—privatization, cut in government spending, etc.—was imposed by international institutions under the name of conditionalities for loans and which have directly affected the masses.[13] The imperialistic character of neoliberal projects can also be seen from the fact that Indian policies are enormously guided by perception of advanced capitalist countries' institutions (e.g. credit rating agencies; imperialist capital) of India's economic prospects and by the massive dependence on the actual flows of imperialist hot money into the country. National sovereignty is an attribute of a democratic republic. The threat to it is caused by the subordination of India's economy to imperialist capital, but this is an issue that those who espouse neoliberalism, including those who call themselves nationalists, do not care about.

## India After the Global Financial Crisis of 2008[14]

In the period since the 2008 global crisis to the present, some of the foregoing trends continue while newer trends manifest themselves. The Indian economy is in a crisis of sorts. India experiences declining growth rate, falling domestic and foreign investment, a depreciating currency, large trade and current accounts deficits, contraction in industrial production, huge stock market losses, and near double-digit inflation.[15] Businesses and academics are talking about India being mired in the possibility, or even actuality, of stagflation (stagnation plus inflation).

The fundamental premise of NEP and neoliberalism is reliance on the private sector to increase exports and earn foreign exchange. And, the fact is that growth of exports is actually falling due to the falling demand for Indian manufactured goods and IT services[16] in the US and Europe, India's most important overseas markets which are reeling under the impacts of the financial crisis. India's merchandise trade deficit shot up from $33.7 billion (5.5 per cent of GDP) in 2004-05 to a gargantuan $190.9 billion (10.6 per cent of GDP) in 2012-13. Thousands of jobs have been eliminated in 'globalized' sectors, including the textile, gem and jewellery, and auto industries and in business processing. Given that these activities are localized, the areas specializing in these are expected to have been hardest hit. The loss of jobs is causing return migration to rural areas which, as mentioned earlier, are already going through a crisis of employment and growth; thus the global economic crisis is exporting the adverse employment effects from urban to rural areas.

Inflation remains at a very high level. Wholesale prices are increasing at a rate of about 8-9 per cent, the most in a decade, and wholesale food prices are rising at a rate of almost 20 per cent. The inflation is because of the combined impact of a shortage of goods, high energy prices (in part caused by withdrawal of government subsidies), and a steep decline in the exchange value of the Indian rupee against the US dollar, which particularly affects the imports (including of oil).

A further measure of the economic slowdown is a sharp decline in investment. New investment proposals fell.[17] Exports are falling in spite of a weak and weakening rupee. By early January 2014, rupee trades at 62 per dollar. It was within a relatively narrow range of around Rs. 45 per dollar for the past decade. Indeed, the Indian rupee was the worst performing major Asian currency in 2011.[18] The immediate trigger for India's currency crisis were the comments made on May 22 by US Federal Reserve Chairman Ben Bernanke that the US central bank may pare back its $85 billion per month bond-buying programme in 2014. Nervous overseas investors responded by pulling more than $11 billion dollars out of Indian stocks and bonds. In the April 2010-March 2011 fiscal year, India received only $19.4 billion in foreign direct investment (FDI), an almost 25 per cent decline from the $25.8 billion recorded in 2009-10. More fundamentally, the rupee's fall has also been fuelled by declines in exports and in both longer-term FDI (Foreign Direct Investment) and the shorter term and more volatile FII (Foreign Institutional Investment), which goes mainly into stocks, bonds and other financial securities. India is not seen as attractive by foreign capital as it was earlier.

Note that a combination of devalued rupee and inflation will not make exports cheaper in dollar terms, so it may not increase exports. On the other hand, the depreciation of the rupee is driving up the cost of India's imports—most importantly of oil (India imports more than three-quarters of the oil it consumes) and of the advanced machinery it needs to equip its export-oriented manufacturing sector—and thereby increasing the country's trade and current accounts deficits while fuelling inflation and dampening economic growth. This in turn makes India less attractive to foreign capital, the inflows of which had driven the growth in the first place.

The decline in foreign exports, a crucial source of foreign currency, is exacerbating the current account deficit (the difference between the country's total exports and imports including monetary transactions). India's CAD (Current Account Deficit) reached $87.8 billion, 4.8 per cent of the Gross Domestic Product, in 2012-13 from a mere $2.5 billion (0.4 per cent of GDP) in 2004-05. India's CAD is now the highest it has been since 1991, and it is one of the highest in the world.

Apart from the threat of a current accounts crisis is the possibility of banking crisis: many companies and especially infrastructure companies, have borrowed excessively from Indian banks and carry an interest burden exceeding their earnings before interest and taxes, and that India's banking system is burdened by a growing number of non-performing loans. (Chandrasekhar, and Ghosh, 2013). Moreover, many of these loans (amounting to more than US $200 billion) are to corporations that have borrowed money in the US and European markets. Since much of the borrowing occurred when the Indian currency was trading at about Rs. 45 to the dollar, the fall in the value of the rupee has effectively boosted the amount borrowed in rupee terms by about 20 per cent.

The economic crisis has led to a rapid swelling of India's budget deficit. The combined deficit for federal and state governments has almost doubled as a proportion of GDP, rising from 5.7 in the 2007-08 fiscal year to a projected 11.1 per cent in 2008-09. The rapid deterioration of India's fiscal position has led the world's major bond-rating agencies to warn that they may soon slash India's credit rating. The fiscal deficit, partly thanks to tax concessions to big business given to encourage them to invest, limits the state's ability to stimulate the stagnating economy.

The upshot of all this is that under the impact of the global financial crisis (and given the dropping demand for crisis-ridden Western markets), India's growth rate fell from 9 per cent in the mid-2000s (and 9.8 per cent in 2007-08) to 6.7 per cent in 2008-09 before recovering somewhat to 7.4 per cent in 2009-10. It was less than 5 per cent in 2012-13, the lowest in a decade. There are several specific reasons for the slowdown. The growth was narrowly based on the consumption expenditure of a tiny layer and not of the majority. The investment boom, enabled by the state offering bribes to business to invest (free resources, tax breaks, etc.) may have created an over-capacity in key sectors which has had a drag effect on growth. Many investment projects did not take off due to legitimate resistance from below and by various corruption scandals, and many infrastructure projects in which a substantial amount of capital has been locked in did not get completed fast enough, and this fact has contributed to slow growth. The delays in environmental clearance for projects are also partly blamed for the slowdown.

## Business Demands, State and Working Class Response

In response to the mounting economic problems, India's business elite has been pressing for the gutting of restrictions on the closure of factories and the contracting-out of work, stepped up privatization and disinvestment, the opening of the retail sector to large foreign multi-brand companies like Walmart, and the imposition of a regressive national goods and services tax. There is even a growing clamour against the National Rural Employment Guarantee on the grounds that it is "unaffordable" and that providing some rural poor with jobs paying little more than a US dollar per day is distorting the "rural labour market." Like its rivals around the world, the Indian bourgeoisie is determined to place the full burden of the capitalist crisis on the working class and rural toilers.

The response of the state to the crisis is full of contradictions. The government made major concessions to big business in three stimulus packages introduced between December 2008 and March 2009, boosting the fiscal deficit[19] (Gunadasa, 2010). The combined central and state government debts have risen to around 80 per cent of GDP. Now the government is imposing these burdens on working people. It is aiming to slash the deficit from 6.9 per cent of GDP in 2009 to 4.1 per cent in 2012-13. The imposition of market pricing on oil products is part of a broader pro-market "reform" agenda being pushed through by the government. The pro-business reforms include privatization of, and disinvestment in, state-owned enterprises, the opening up of multi-brand retail and other sectors of the economy to foreign investment, and cuts to energy- and fertilizer-price subsidies.[20] Also, the government approved measures to further open the country's economy to foreign capital.

Opening up the economy to foreign capital further contributes to the economy's dependence on hot money which is one reason for the crisis itself. Keynesian fiscal stimulus measures can only be limited as the funds at the disposal of the Indian government hardly allow it to deliver much fiscal stimulus. Although India's central bank has been intervening periodically, including in early January 2014, selling dollars so as to drive up the value of the rupee. But the RBI's reserves have fallen to around $290 billion from an all-time high of $321 billion in 2011. This is barely enough for 7 months of imports and is down significantly from 2008, when the RBI possessed enough reserves for 15 months of imports.[21] The other financial "tool" available to the RBI to bolster the value of the rupee is to increase domestic interest rates. But restricting credit would dampen economic activity under conditions where India's economy is already suffering from slow growth. Capital controls were also imposed but these would be counterproductive because the limits on Indians transferring assets overseas backfired, as they caused foreign investors, fearful that they might be next, to withdraw funds from India.

The government has also responded to the sharp fall in India's economic growth rate to less than 5 per cent by slashing social spending and accelerating the implementation of pro-market reforms.

The working masses have suffered the most. A recent study found that between 1991 and 2011 the real income of workers increased by less than 1 per cent. And hunger stalks rural India with a majority of India's children stunted and malnourished. The working class has gone on strikes against many of these interventions but the strike has often been used by the working class leaders/misleaders more as oppositional politics: "oppositional" politics that is entirely within the confines of the political parties and political structures of the bourgeoisie. There has been scarcely any attempt to go beyond trade unionist thinking or trade unionist action to launch class struggle proper, that is, struggle against the social-political order itself. All the major trade unions that called the strike are affiliated to political parties, including the two major communist parties, that have been instrumental in the implementation of pro-market reforms themselves and have limited legitimacy in the eyes of ordinary workers, and are hardly taken seriously by the elite.

## Conclusion

Obsessed with the idea of 9 per cent economic growth rate, the elite, whether it is from this or that political party, treats economic development issues (which are conflated with economic growth) as a matter of national security. This is ominous, smacking of authoritarianism. Any ideological-political resistance to NEP is not be tolerated because such resistance is apparently against the interest of the nation, or it is against common sense.

Whatever the fate of the rupee in the future, it is evident that India is in the maelstrom of the world capitalist crisis. Underlying the financial problems of emerging market countries such as India was and is the absence of any genuine recovery in the real economies of the advanced capitalist countries. The coming period will see a rapid intensification of the class struggle as the Indian elite and international capital seek to force the working class and rural poor to pay for the bankruptcy and irrationality of the profit system. Without high growth the profits of the private business houses, it will be impossible to absorb the tens of millions who will be joining the labour force in the coming years. The number of under-employed and unemployed will continue to grow as a result of population growth (even if it has thankfully dropped). It will also grow as a result of the bourgeoisie's drive to engage in primitive accumulation and thus displace petty producers in agriculture and handicrafts and the large number of family-owned shops with production and commercial firms organized along capitalist lines.

The crisis of the Indian economy is increasingly resembling the 1991 situation. The year 1991 is and is not like 2014. At that time India's foreign currency reserves fell to a level barely enough to cover a few weeks of imports. This prompted the Indian elite, which was politically divided, to turn to the International Monetary Fund for an emergency loan which forced India to abandon state-led economic development. Unlike in 1991, India may now have foreign currency reserves of six to seven months. However, India's economy is much more connected to the world capitalist economy today than in 1991, and world capitalism is now riven by the greatest crisis since the Great Depression. While the global economic crisis shows no sign of genuine resolution (and another one might come soon), India's political and economic elite's ability to address its own crisis within the territorial boundaries of the nation-state seems to be limited. The Indian elite facing a choice between a) trying to boost economic growth by letting the rupee slide still further, thereby fuelling growth-sapping inflation and b) defending the currency by tightening credit and thereby further squeezing economic growth. And in the background looms the threat of a rapid depletion of India's reserves as foreign capital spurns a crisis-ridden economy.

Workers in India, as workers around the world, must engage in a struggle not just against this or that political regime/ party (or government), not just against this or that leader, and not just for this or that small concession, which can be given today and taken away tomorrow. On the basis of these partial struggles, and independently of bourgeois forces, they must engage in a political struggle against capitalism, as it exists in India (mainly as a low-wage-platform of the imperialist system) and for the reorganization of society. Their aim should be to establish a system of production, the dominant focus of which is to meet the need of millions of ordinary people constituting the majority of the nation, rather than to merely produce profits for a few. Militant industrial action in defence of jobs, against casualization and for basic rights must be developed. But they must be developed as part of an independent ideological and political offensive of the working class for a workers' and poor peasants' government. The working class in towns and cities and surrounding villages must rally the poor peasants and other oppressed sections of society (millions of aboriginal people) under its leadership in a struggle against big business, the landowners and moneylenders and their political and intellectual representatives. What is necessary is a mass revolutionary party that is not electoralist and that begins to prosecute the struggle not only to destroy remnants of feudal landlordism but also to overthrow the profit-driven system controlled by Indian and foreign moneybags, and establish a workers and small-scale producers' government in India as a part of such a process in South Asia and globally. The enormous ability of Indians to work and India's massive natural resources should effectively belong to those who do the manual and intellectual work, should be controlled by them, and should be used to satisfy their material and cultural needs, and not to satisfy a tiny minority's insatiable appetite for profit, an appetite that is met with massive assistance from the leaders of major political parties, top government officials and bureaucrats of major trade unions.

## Notes

1. They include: self-employed small-scale manufacturers and traders; and those in well-paid occupations with a high salary generating a saving and with some control over their workplace.
2. Note that the book does not deal with the important topic of ecological change.
3. This section draws on Das (2012c).
4. Often members of the business class or their paid advisors are directly writing policy documents of the government. If one needs an example of the privatization of the public power, here is one.
5. This does not mean that the way in which capitalists' interests are reflected in NEP can be entirely reduced to their interests. When these interests are mediated by the state, there is some role for relatively autonomous actions of the state (including electoral compulsion in India), which colours the ways in which NEP meets capitalists' interests.
6. The next 7 lines are based on Basu and Das (2013).
7. Net capital inflows as a percentage of GDP increased from 2 per cent in 1998-2003 to almost 9 per cent in 2007-08.
8. This means that 90 per cent of Indians own less than a quarter of the country's wealth. India has the fastest rate of growth of US dollar billionaires amongst major countries of the world, while the bread-earner earns Rs. 10,000 or less per month in 2011 in 90 per cent of all the families in the country. The real wage for the bulk of India's workforce was, on an average, Rs. 146 per day in 1991, which increased to merely Rs. 272 in 2004 (which is really not an increase, if inflation is taken into account). While per capita GDP increased from $ 310 before neoliberalism to $ 1,500 in recent times, such an increase says nothing about the growing inequality between the top 1 per cent or top 10 per cent, and the rest.
9. 'The state under neoliberalism...actively promotes an increase in the share of surplus value in the hands of domestic and foreign corporates...' (Patnaik, 2010).
10. It has dropped from 2.85 in 1993-94 to 1.9 per cent in 2000-2001 (Patnaik, 2007: 155).
11. It is not just that many roads are toll roads. It is also the case that people need money to pay for a bus ticket in order to be able to use the roads. If people do not have well-paying regular employment, development as *bijli*, *sadak* and *pani*, etc. means little.

12. In fact, the state apparatus is increasingly occupied by pro-market ideologues and neoliberal technocrats and indeed by business people themselves. This signifies the neoliberalization and technocratization of the state apparatus.
13. It is also interesting that exactly the same sort of measures have been undertaken in imperialist countries themselves in the interest of their top '1-5 per cent' which have impacted their own '95-99 per cent'. Neoliberalism—onslaught of capital on the toiling masses—is the thread that links the toiling masses of the world, although these masses in the poorer countries such as India are affected far more than in richer countries.
14. This section is, more or less, based on a paper I wrote for Canadian Dimension in early 2014 (Das, 2014c; see also Das, 2015).
15. Apparently, an annual growth rate of 9 per cent is necessary to absorb into its workforce tens of millions of working- and middle-class job seekers.
16. India is the most important site of IT-enabled offshore operations for the US and British banks that have been at the centre of the world financial meltdown.
17. It fell from 45 per cent in 2011 to a five-year low of $209.2 billion. This compares with $376 billion in 2010. In order to check price-rise, the Reserve Bank of India raised the interest rate 13 times between March 2010 and October 2011. Even after the inflation rate declined, it was reluctant to lower interest rates (partly) because of the recent rapid depreciation of the Indian rupee and fear of capital flight. (In 2016, whether or not to reduce the interest rate has been a reason for the tension between the central bank and the central government, with the central bank being in favour of not lowering the interest rate, in order to check inflation).
18. The depreciation of the rupee—like that in other emerging markets—came due to fears of European sovereign debt defaults and the possible unravelling of the Eurozone led investors to stampede to the US dollar.
19. It increased from from 2.6 per cent of gross domestic product (GDP) in 2007-08 to 6.7 per cent in the 2009-10 fiscal year.
20. Even as retail price inflation has risen at 10 per cent or more, the government has imposed further energy price increases (Gunadasa, 2010).
21. In contrast, the Chinese regime has accumulated a mountain of $3.2 trillion in foreign currency reserves.

# 3

# Neoliberalism, Agrarian Crisis, and Farmers' Suicides

A major effect of the profit-driven system in India is the fact that the very people who produce food and raw materials from agriculture for capitalist industries do not themselves live a life of security and happiness. Indeed, thousands of farmers have been killing themselves. Between 1995 and 2016, more than 330,000 farmers have committed suicide. The rate at which farmers commit suicide is higher than the rate for the general population. This Chapter provides some preliminary statistical analysis of the phenomenon in the light of an alternative theoretical approach taken to the topic.

## How to Think About Farmers' Suicides?

Many writers say that farmers' suicides happen because of factors such as the withdrawal of state subsidies and indebtedness. Such a view is not wrong, but taken on its own, it is deficient. In fact, a problem with much of the existing thinking on the issue of farmers' suicides (FS) is that it is treated more or less as a rural issue, or an agrarian issue. Also the underlying assumption of much work is that the state has the power to genuinely solve the problem. Thus much of the research suffers from a lack of thorough conceptual sensitivity. Offered here is a short alternative framework which treats FS as a part of a wider system, the system of capitalism. This system is determined by the law of value as an international process:

this is the idea that producers in all regions and countries have to produce at a competitive price (see Das, 2013 for more details). Producers not being able to produce at an average cost become economically unviable in a market system, and their cost of production can be uncompetitive despite the fact that as individuals they are industrious and enterprising.

All small-scale producers are vulnerable. Farmers are particularly vulnerable because of nature-dependent and geographically dispersed and relatively small-scale character of their production. In other words: when business owners do not make 'enough' money, they can lose their business. The poorer 'strata' among them (e.g. farmers) are more vulnerable to losing their business, and sometimes, to losing their lives. On the other hand, some businesses—e.g. lenders, seeds companies—make money.

Farmers are facing a major contradiction: that is between near-stagnant revenue/income and rising costs. This contradiction makes farmers vulnerable to indebtedness including in usurious form, and to social humiliation, caused by their inability to pay back loans and by the potential of them losing their land. After all, land is not merely a means of production; it has some symbolic value. These processes are compounded by the fact of the absence of a strong counter-mechanism or support network in the form of, for example, an anti-capitalist movement in situ, a fact which adds to farmers' desperation. Such desperation has been an ongoing process, which, beyond a limit, compels farmers to take their own lives.

So, the overall approach here is framed by the law of value, which stresses international competitiveness and differentials in (labour) productivity, and by the state and associated processes in relation to this law. The two main causal mechanisms then are: agri-globalization,[1] and relative neoliberalization of the capitalist state. Both are aspects of the multi-scalar capitalist system. The following points seek to elabourate the approach.

1. To produce something in a given amount of labour time embodied in living labour and in dead labour (e.g. machines, tools, processed raw materials) is needed, whether the thing

is produced on a farm or in a factory. The labour time that a factory or a farm needs in order to produce what it produces must be close to the average for the industry of which such a farm/factory is a part. Roughly, this is the law of value, in technical language. In the language of price, the cost of production of a commodity on a farm or a factory must be competitive; it must be close to the socially average cost, the cost that holds in the entire industry within which the farm or a factory operates.

2. There is an economy of scale: when commodities are produced in bulk, the cost of production per commodity unit tends to be reduced. So smaller owners are generally inefficient owners in the long term. When they appear to be efficient, often that apparent efficiency exists because of the intense level of self-exploitation (for example, farmers under-feed themselves and their animals) as well as over-exploitation of the natural resources. Their cost of production, including the imputed cost of family labour, is more than the average cost of production for the industry.

3. The law of value is ultimately an international process. The cost of production of a farm or a factory in a country is compared to that in other countries and across the globe (or across a bloc of countries trading with one another). Such a comparison happens behind the backs of those who own farms or factories. There is an increasing pressure on all producers to cut the cost of production and to force the cost of production of every producing unit to the socially average cost. The increasing use of technologies (both biological technology including modern seeds and mechanical technology, including machines) must be seen as a part of this process.

4. Social or non-market intervention can aim to bridge the gap between the two values (two costs): individual and social. This role can be played sometimes and in some places by the state and by institutions of the social economy, including philanthropy, NGOs, and self-help groups.

If a farmer is commercially producing cotton at or above the social value (if her/his cost is more than the average cost of cotton in the country), the state can ensure that the gap between the social value and the individual value is minimized, so that the farmer can remain in business in spite of being (somewhat) inefficient. Till the early 1990s (and in some cases earlier), the state, to some extent, by subsidizing farm inputs and by guaranteeing some kind of remunerative price for farm outputs, had been performing this bridging role for farmers (as well as other kinds of property owners).

5. But the state itself (like other similar institutions) is increasingly subject to the law of value, because it itself is dependent on value creation and value circulation. The state cannot continue to play the role of 'value-matching' for too long. It cannot do so especially after capitalism—its law of value—has become, in reality, more and more globalized. There is increasing pressure on the state in India (and other less developed countries) from imperialist institutions to stop playing the bridging role so that a 'level playing field' is created internationally (it is another matter that commodity producers in powerful countries are often protected by their own states).

6. This has resulted in the law of value acting as if it were a natural force, destroying inefficient property owners or at least economically weakening them. If the cost of producing a commodity or a service is consistently above the average, that unit can be in trouble.

7. The so-called agrarian crisis is, to a large extent, a crisis of smaller property owners, under the rule of capital as a global social relation—i.e. under the rule of the law of value. Not only that. The small-scale nature of production in agriculture is compounded by the fact that small-scale owners are often forced to lose their land and to experience adverse terms of trade against farming (the cost of the inputs they buy rises faster than the rise of the prices of what they sell). Besides, in rural areas, the cost of healthcare (as well as the cost of other things farmers need) is also rising for the families of farmers, and this factor adversely affects their income.

8. The other side of the agrarian crisis is the crisis of livelihood of workers who are involved in production. As

the imperative of cost cutting gets strong and globalized, there is not only a tendency towards unemployment/under-employment (in spite of palliatives such as employment guarantee schemes). Such an imperative also leads to a situation where wages paid by small capitals are hardly adequate for a decent life. Rural labour, including that employed intermittently by rural small capitals (including non-farm business), is a part of the expanding reserve army of the world, which allows the super-exploitation of those who are hired. In other words: super-exploitation of rural labour is a part of the agrarian crisis, which, in turn, is a part of the crisis of small capitals. The agrarian crisis is not entirely about farmers and peasants. It is also about rural labour. It is not about agrarian or rural capitalism. It is about capitalism tout court.

In other words, there is a global tendency towards class differentiation, towards concentration and centralization, and towards competition between more and less efficient producers. This process includes a) a process of the expansion of the global working class, which is living a precarious life, b) a process of smaller owners gradually going out of business, and c) a process of some people increasingly controlling more and more of society's material resources (including the land of erstwhile owners).

Because there are small capitals—or small-scale property owners, including those who may employ a few wage workers—in all countries of the world (rich and poor), there is a crisis of small property ownership everywhere in the world.

9. The globalization of the law of value—the law of competitiveness—is mediated by various factors (including the operation of self-help groups), which can modify the law in specific localities, producing spatial unevenness. But the law itself is undoubtedly operational.

The aim of the remainder of the Chapter is to show temporal trends and geographical variation in FS, and shed light on some of the 'correlates' of FS, within the overall framework briefly outlined. Within this framework, there are specific issues which can be expressed as 'variables', which are indicative of definite processes.[2] The question of rural labour will be abstracted from in what follows.

## A Brief Empirical Examination of Farmers' Suicides

Farmers' suicides, like most things in society, are geographically concentrated. There are several aspects of geographical distribution. In terms of absolute numbers: 90 per cent are from 10 major states and 75 per cent of the cases are from five states located in South India: Kerala, Karnataka, Andhra Pradesh, Maharashtra and Tamil Nadu. Between 1995 and 2004, farmers' suicides (FS) have increased from 10,730 to 18,241 a year. Between 1996 and 2004 (the peak year), FS grew by 32 per cent, and this period, coincides with the period when BJP was in power (except for a few months). The overall rate of increase appears to have declined slightly, although how much of that decline is because of the way FS is counted is a different matter.

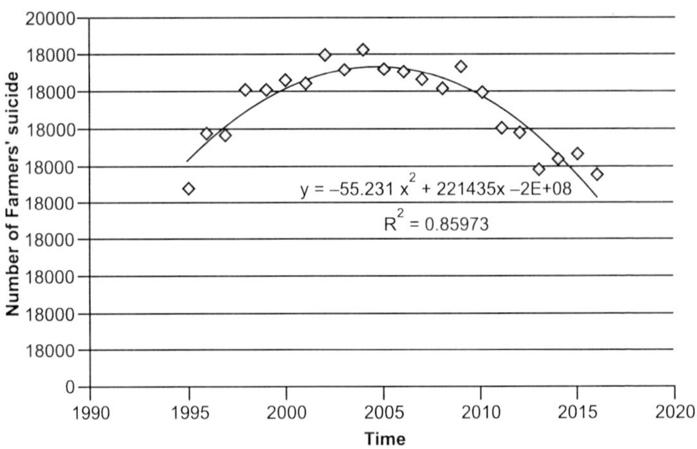


Figure 2: Trends in Farmers' Suicides in India: 1995-2016

*Sources:* The figure is constructed on the basis of the farmers' suicides data taken from different sources: Mishra, 2014; Waghmare, 2017; Bera, 2018

As mentioned, the phenomenon of FS can only be explained within a multi-scalar framework which takes into account globalization of Indian agriculture and the associated question of how competitive this sector is, as well as the declining ability of the state to mitigate the effects of international competition.

The costs of production of farm produce have been rising. One reason is that there is a relative reduction in the state's subsidy for farm inputs, including fertilizer. Fertilizer subsidy has changed by minus 7.8 per cent between 1995 and 2010. It is declining at an increasing rate. This reduction in social (=state) support for production has contributed to the rising cost of private production.

In fact, the FS trend follows the trend in the overall government expenditure for agriculture (Figure 3). In the market also, the cost of other inputs (e.g. seeds) has been increasing. Not just that. There has been an increase in rural living costs, including the cost of healthcare, which is increasingly privatized. On the other hand, farmers' income has been decreasing. Share of agriculture and allied sectors in GDP has dropped to 13 per cent in 2012, while the farm dependent population remains at 58 per cent. Crop failures are regular due to drought, which is happening once every 3 years or so. The effects of drought are severe because of the state's failure to provide adequate irrigation facilities.[3] Seventy per cent of farmland still depends on monsoons.

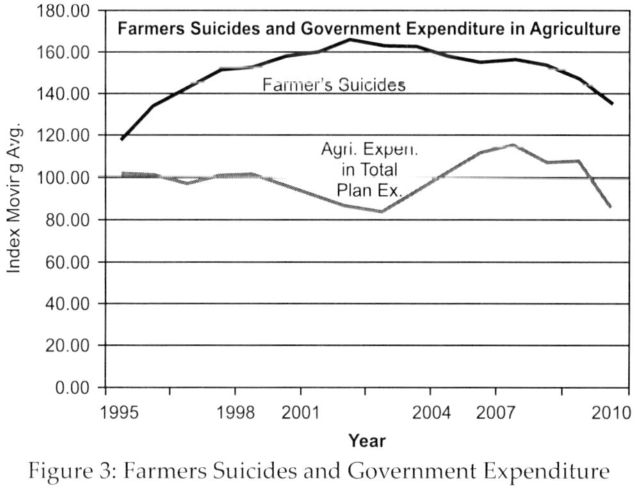


Figure 3: Farmers Suicides and Government Expenditure

Farm prices are relatively low. One reason is that the government is not buying farm products at a remunerative price as it used to do before. Also there is the issue of agri-globalization. With import liberalization, cheap and subsidized foreign products flood the market, leading to the fall in domestic prices. Non-food crops (e.g. cotton, coffee, pepper, cardamom) are especially affected as they are more commercialized and are more export-oriented. So some of the areas with a higher proportion of land which is used for these crops experience more FS.

Farm productivity in India is relatively low in the global context, and the state's withdrawal of input subsidies contributes to this, which is adversely affecting farmers' international competitiveness. The extent of mechanization that can increase labour productivity is much less in India than in advanced countries. For example, the US has twice the number of tractors per 100 square kilometres of arable land that India has (256 vs 128). Productivity differential is also enormous between India and advanced countries such as the US (see Figure 4). If farmers in India, most of whom operate on a small scale, appear to be competitive, it is more or less because of their self-exploitation.[4]

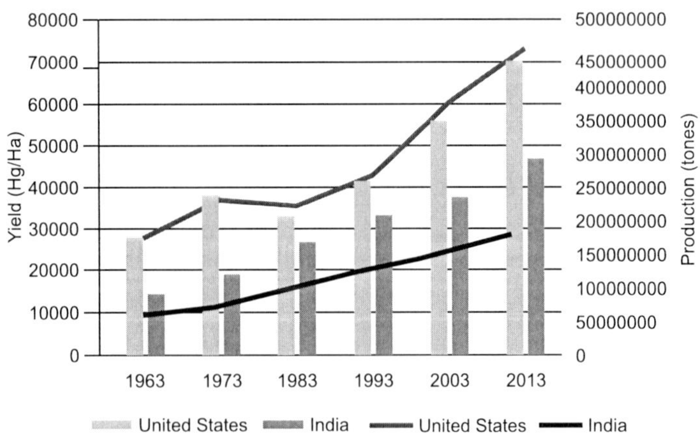


Figure 4: Total Cereal Production (tonnes) and Yield (Hg/Ha) in India and the United States

As a result of all these factors, farmers are experiencing a high level of indebtedness. An important aspect of this is the fact that because of the decline in credit facilities from government sources, there is greater reliance on private-lenders who lend at usurious rates. Increasing indebtedness along with the threat of the loss of their land, which is a source of economic and symbolic value, to more successful farmers and/or money-lenders (and in many cases land speculators)[5], is compelling many farmers to commit suicide. In some areas, farmers committing suicide are 3-4 times more indebted than those who have not committed suicide. This means that economic distress caused by the difficulties discussed above are being translated into an emotional trauma among the vulnerable sub-groups, and long-term emotional trauma triggers suicides.

## Conclusion

If the agrarian crisis is a crisis of small-scale property ownership (and a crisis of livelihood of the labouring class), a crisis caused by the capitalist relations operating increasingly at a global level, it follows that the long-term resolution of such a crisis requires concerted multi-scale political mobilization on the part of labour and peasants/farmers against global capitalist relations to establish a society where resources, including land, are used in an ecologically sound manner for the benefit of all human beings of the world.

It is important to stress that FS is a part of a wider system, the system of capitalist production and exchange, which is governed by the law of value. This law is a multi-scalar process. But in the final instance, it is an international process. By putting pressure on local and national 'economies' to be internationally competitive, this process can potentially undermine the conditions of small-scale producers engaged in commodity production. This same process also limits the ability of the state to protect these producers in any significant and sustainable manner.

Chronic indebtedness—a debt trap—caused by rising input prices and inadequate farm-revenue, happening in a context of increasing exposure to international competitiveness and low farm productivity is a root cause of the problem of FS. Farmers' suicides signify a more general phenomenon: the crisis of reproduction of small-scale property owners including small-scale capitalists, in global capitalism. Farmers' suicides are happening in a country which is increasingly run by, and on behalf of, a small class of owners of big business (domestic and foreign), which is supported by corrupt, and subservient politicians/officials. FS signifies a form of violence committed by the political-economic system which cares for profit more than for human need and human life.[6] Tacking FS and its underlying causes would need a massive democratic organization of farmers and of labourers, under the political-intellectual leadership of the latter, to demand a system in which the profit-motive is subordinated to human need, and where food and means of production of food (such as land, machines and seeds, etc.) are not treated as commodities that are bought and sold for a profit. And small-scale owners, whether in farming or outside farming and whether in poorer countries such as India or richer countries such as the US, are experiencing a similar squeeze on their incomes. Therefore, small-scale producers of richer and poorer countries have a common interest in opposing the profit-driven system that aims to treat everything as a commodity and that treats farming as a means to make a profit for a tiny minority.

## Notes

1. This refers to the operation of the capitalist system in agriculture at the global level.
2. The preliminary empirical analysis here is based on the statistical analysis at national/sub-national scales. But a proper analysis requires that it happens at more local scales and that statistical analysis be combined with qualitative analysis. The statistical work in this Chapter was partly conducted by Dr. Mohanakumar of the Institute of Development Studies, Jaipur. Dr. Mohanakumar constructed Figure 3. Figure 4 was constructed for me by my PhD student, Mizhar Mikati at York University.
3. Indeed, public infrastructure investment in rural areas is falling while the state is spending millions on infrastructure for big business.

4. It should be noted that small-scale producers in farming in advanced countries such as Canada and the US are also vulnerable to competition from large-scale producers. And to the extent that farming—including that practised by small-sale owners—has been competitive in advanced countries, it is not just because its level of use of technology is high, increasing farm productivity, as compared to that in the less developed countries. The level of government subsidy for farmers in the advanced countries has been much higher than in poorer countries such as India.
5. If farmers in an area are not producing enough revenue at a given point of time, they are vulnerable to their land being bought up by speculators/developers, etc.
6. Interestingly, the Indian states ruled by the Left are among those where FS rate is high. This raises the question about the Left regimes and indeed about social democracy and its underlying theory of political economy, and about the limits to what a Left regime can do to help small-scale producers in a capitalist society.

# 4

# Neoliberalism, the Education Market, Civil Servants and the State

Neoliberalism—which is the short form for neoliberal capitalism and which we have talked about earlier—is affecting all sectors and spheres of life. One of these is the educational landscape of the 'new India'. Education is increasingly a commodity, in reality and in the minds of millions of people. It is a commodity which private enterprises produce and sell for considerable profit. And it is a commodity for ordinary people: they buy it—i.e. they buy the skills that are saleable in the job-market. They hope to sell their skills to recoup their investment.

The ubiquitous coaching (or tutoring) institutes form an important part of the market in education. Partly because of the collapse of the formal education structure (e.g. high-quality public sector institutions), they are mushrooming to prepare students for the college exams and for various entrance exams (see Appendix 1). In this Chapter, I wish to briefly discuss a particular kind of coaching institutes. These are the ones that prepare civil service aspirants for the competitive exams. They are the exams that people take in order to qualify for various high-level jobs in the government sector.

## Civil Service Coaching Institutes: What are They and Why do They Exist?

For the civil service coaching institutes to exist, there must be many people who are interested in civil services. Every year the Union Public Service Commission (UPSC) of the Government of India conducts an examination (Civil Services Exam) to recruit candidates to fill various government posts such as Indian Administrative Service, Indian Foreign Service, Indian Police Service, Indian Revenue Service, and so on. Typically, more than 400,000 people appear for the UPSC exams every year, in recent times. The fact that a large number of people are interested in civil service exams indeed creates a demand for the private, for-profit coaching institutes. The instructors in these institutes make young minds memorize this bit of fact about WTO or that bit of fact about the height of mountains in the world, or Article number X or Y in the Indian Constitution, and so on. People with higher degrees, for whom learning is merely a means of making money, become involved in the educational business, including as owners and managers of the business, euphemistically known as institutes, centres, etc. There are often college/university teachers who provide coaching service for a fee on a part-time basis. People write notebooks for civil service aspirants, which must have questionable analytical/intellectual content, given the motivation of both the writers and readers of such material, which is anything but intellectual. There is hardly any regulation of the quality of the teaching work conducted in these and similar other tutoring institutes. Many of the people involved in the coaching business are likely to be 'mediocre' fellows, 'mediocre', judged from the standpoint of intellectual quality: a piece of writing has superior intellectual quality if it promotes, among other things, an understanding of society and nature a) that is explanatory and critical of various inequalities and power relations, and b) that is solidly informed by relevant philosophies and theories and by reasoned argument backed by evidence. High quality intellectual ideas do not take what merely appears to be true as true and do not treat facts and information as raw data: they relate one thing to another, and say something general about a society and about nature (and their interaction), and so on.

Not only this. Many of the people in the coaching business are those who themselves have tried but failed to succeed in the competitions for civil service type jobs (for whatever reasons). In other words, people who have neither succeeded in competing for civil service posts nor in the academic world of learning coach people on how to learn things to succeed in the exams. It is also interesting that some of the teachers in these money-grabbing coaching institutes talk about pedagogy, learning style, etc. Institutes charge an excessive amount making them lucrative. One wonders who really can afford the kind of money they charge. The bottom 70 per cent barely lives, so it quietly leaves the sphere of life where lofty aspirations exist and which coaching institutes, among others, pedal. The civil service coaching institutes—the civil service knowledge industry—really contribute to the circulation of status, power and money in the 'top 20-30 per cent circle'. Sons and daughters of this top stratum can afford to take time off and spend money, buying the services of the so-called institutes, and compete for the few positions. If success comes, it is not too difficult to retrieve the money invested and to make huge amounts of money on top of the initial investment. It should be noted that central civil servants, who barely constitute 5 per cent of all government employees of the central government, are generally drawn from urban areas and from the relatively privileged class, caste and other backgrounds.[1] Many of those people who appear for the civil service exams or succeed have an undergraduate degree or if they have a higher degree, much of their learning is simply motivated by the desire to do well in the exams (as opposed to a desire to learn and enjoy the beauty of knowledge and deploy it in the interest of the majority). Interestingly, ideas emanating from these people form an important part of the intellectual basis for policy formation. I am, of course, generalizing, and am abstracting from the fact that there are inevitably people among the civil servants who could have had an excellent career in research and who could equally engage in superior quality knowledge production but chose not to.

## Why Such a Craze for Civil Service Exams?: From Civil Services to the Nature of the State

Individuals in society do certain things and think in certain ways, and thus exercise their human agency. Undoubtedly one person does things differently from another person. That is also true. But on close reflection, one finds that what appears to be an individual way of doing/thinking, and underlying the inter-individual differences and all the so-called unique actions and ways of thinking, is something that is actually very social (and systemic). This social cannot be reduced to the individual, even if the social 'emerges' out of, and is reproduced/changed by, what individuals do. To do certain things and to think in certain ways, there must be social conditions which exist independently of what individuals do and think. I am free to open a bank account, to want to save by working hard and put my savings in a savings account, and I am free to encash a cheque given to me by someone. But for all these things to happen, there has to be money, which is clearly not my creation, and there has to be a banking system, and all the rules that shape how the system works and what is the interest rate, etc., none of which I, as an individual, have much power to control. Similarly, the coaching institutes exist and work because there are people interested in taking the civil service exams. The next question is: why are so many young and bright people—including people who have spent years obtaining a degree in engineering and medicine and at the public expense—interested in civil service exams anyway? In the UK, or in Canada or the US, the so-called civil servants do not receive the kind of attention that they do in India. The best minds there become lawyers, doctors, engineers, professors, researchers in the private sector, and so on. Serious scholars hardly opt for a career in the civil services in these economically developed countries. Why is the Indian case different? One can say that given that there are not many jobs for the educated people, a civil service job is a job. But a civil service job is not merely a job. There is more to the craze than the fact that it is just a job. There are many causes for the craze, which have all got to do with the nature of the society itself and of the state which is a part of that society.

More or less sharing the world view of the wealthiest (and often upper caste views), civil servants and their political masters (=politicians) manage the common affairs of the propertied class, including the fractions within this class that have a dominance on the basis of caste and ethnicity, and increasingly, religion. This fact of civil servants' shared world-view and their subservient role in relation to the economic and political elite, is a cause of the power of civil servants. They also look after individual interests of powerful competing fractions of this class. That is also a source of their power.[2] So the power of the civil servants over ordinary citizens and their power to do things in their own interest (including out of turn privileges) has a social cause: it is connected to the class character (and, more concretely, the class-caste character) of the broader society. Their subservience to the property-owners and the political leaders, and thus their powerlessness, is manifested as their power over the masses. Within this common framework, which applies to India and other societies, do we have to see the power of civil servants in India.

Before the late 1980s, many civil servants achieved their status of powerful people by working for local landlords and kings, whose extra-economic importance has diminished somewhat now. Earlier, their power also came from their ability to manage the common affairs just mentioned and from their ability to favour this or that business house (who will get what concession/subsidy from the state) and who can bypass which formal regulation. If a government regulation is there (for example, one that disallows the use of child labour in a sector), civil servants can receive monetary compensation from the business class, to look the other way: a certain part of the extra profit that a business person makes by violating the regulation is shared with the civil servants (who probably share a part of the bribe with their political masters, in order to receive protection from them). Civil servants and politicians can also 'sell' a given policy to meet the specific needs of a given fraction of the capitalist class by presenting that policy as being in the interest of economic development, and in the interest of the nation. What has changed since the 1990s, i.e. since the neoliberal turn has happened?[3] Increasingly, civil servants in India are overseeing a market system, where animal spirits are highly encouraged, right from the Prime Minister's office. They need to ensure the success of the market system during their formal tenure (and after retirement, when they work as so-called consultants for this or that business). Now as before their power comes from their ability to favour the business class as such vis-a-vis the working masses. In particular, much of their power now comes from the ability to dispose of public assets to private players at a throwaway price, and from making land and other natural resources available to the business class that are taken away from unorganized peasants. Their power also comes from connecting this or that fraction of the business class to the international circuit of capital and powerful foreign states (and vice versa) on favourable terms, and so on. In playing this sort of 'compradore' role, they are helped by the fact that they may have worked for international institutions and have connections with them.

Bureaucrats' power comes from the very character of the capitalism that India (like similar less developed countries) has: bureaucrats 'oversee' a type of capitalist production which is not only based on a massive amount of dispossession of small-scale property owners but also on the regime of low wages and long hours. It is not a capitalism where in the sphere of production the main method of surplus appropriation is based on systemic technological change aimed at increasing productivity of labour. The dominance of this form of capitalism has traditionally marked the more developed countries.[4] And a regime of capitalism that is based on dispossession of small-scale producers and on business owners making people work for low wages and long hours, is hardly conducive to very democratic relations between state (officials) and citizens. When profits come more or less from the naked exhaustion of the body of direct producers whose very basic needs remain unmet (or from their dispossession) rather than from increased productivity of their labour, the coercive relation on the part of the state, the state of the capitalist class, tends to be everywhere.[5]

This is a society where, partly thanks to the kind of ('under-developed') capitalism it has, there are massive (near-) starvation, mass illiteracy, and enormous inequality in the means of consumption of what is required for a decent living. Such a situation, along with the absence of effective people's resistance against injustice, promote what is effectively an undemocratic state in its daily functioning (albeit disguised under democratic clothes). There is indeed a direct association between increasing inequality and increasing authoritarianism of the state, in all societies, including India.[6] By virtue of its location in a poverty-stricken class divided society, where the direct producers also experience enormous caste and gender oppression and lack basic skills such as literacy, the state has much authoritarian power, some of which it acquired during colonial times for the purpose of carrying out the orders of the imperialist masters and keeping the 'natives' in check. This power—the power of the state—is exercised by agents of the state: the civil servants (and their political masters). Ordinary masses bear the brunt of it.[7]

While officials' power comes from their power to intervene on behalf of, and at the behest of business class people and landlords, their power, dialectically seen, has another source: their role in relation to the working masses. When the super-exploited masses create some 'trouble' (for example, when they speak against exploitation and oppression, when they try to form a union or engage in a slight protest), the civil servants as servants of the wealthy people arrive with all their administrative might, including abuse of their power. The economic elite uses civil servants as their foot soldiers to keep the masses under control, not only through naked physical and administrative force but also through deception, lies, trickery, mystification, etc. They have to constantly 'tell' people that elections, and not protests/strikes, are a way of showing disapproval of a government and that government offices (e.g.

collector's office or a police station) are there basically to help ordinary people, that low-income toilers and rich property-owners are all equal in the eyes of the law, that the profit-driven market system benefits everyone, that industrialization is in the interest of all, and so on, or they (civil servants) have to work on a day-to-day basis in line with these principles. In so far as one needs useful ideas (discourses) to perform their role, civil servants are well supported/ served by another group: so-called 'intellectuals' (people in academic, media, etc., including those who have coached them in the coaching institutes). Coercion and trickery, etc. are not the civil servants' only role, which gives them power over the masses. In a society where economic and social development is a massive unfulfilled need, having to prostrate before the officials as a means of getting a few crumbs makes officials the semi-kings ('mai-baap') that they are. A colonial inheritance, this system of power relations between civil servants and ordinary people, is one that serves the capitalist system as a whole very well. It supplements the role of the police and army as well as private armies of property-owners and paramilitary forces and vigilante groups, associated with certain social-cultural organizations, in keeping the masses in check. In fact, given the increasing influence of fascistic ideology on civil servants, they can and do look the other way when ordinary people are under physical attack from groups subscribing to that ideology.

What we have is a structure of relations among any elements (see the Figure below). The practice and discourse of the pursuit of quick money and indeed fetishization of money and money-making-at-any-cost;[8] a system of capitalist production based on a regime of low-wages and long hours; the need for the state to play a mediating role in relation to the market relations and (global) capitalism; the need for an undemocratic governance; privatization and cultural devaluation of education, and continuing colonial legacy/ mentality. They produce an interesting structure, which operates through many contingent mechanisms. One of these are the so-called coaching institutes (preparing people for civil services exams). This structure is an oppressive one. More specifically, civil servants as they operate on the ground are one of the most important obstacles to the exercise of democratic rights by ordinary citizens. And civil servants exercising the power of the state as a structure-in-itself are one of the strongest fortresses around state power vis-a-vis workers, peasants, adivasis and lower-caste poor people.

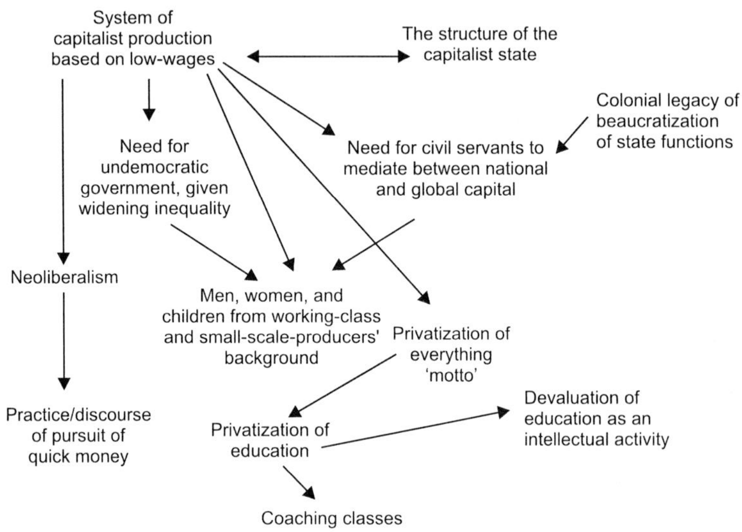


Figure 5: Civil Servants and Coaching for Civil Services Examination: A Structural View

## Radical Civil Servants: An Oxymoron

What about radicals? Like liberals, many of them perhaps believe that by being a civil servant they can help the poor. Many people believe in the semi-social-democratic illusion that the state itself is an arena of class struggle and that pro-poor civil servants can genuinely do significant things to help a large number of poor and needy people.[9] It is undeniable that sometimes a collector can build a road or provide some short-term employment to a few people or take action against a predatory contractor. The civil servants—not as persons but as occupiers of positions in the capitalist state structure and as bearers of the capitalist class relations—are, and must be, a major object of intellectual and political critique, from the standpoint of ordinary citizens' interests and lives. One cannot see how people can become civil servants with the aim of significantly helping the poor majority, who are precisely the sorts of people who must be exploited, dispossessed, dominated and oppressed by the capitalist class to accumulate its wealth, the class in whose fundamental interests the civil servants must work. Is it not the case that: the class character of society places extremely strong limits within which the state as a structure has to work. Is it not the case that the state structure in turn puts strong limits within which agents of the state (e.g. civil servants and politicians) themselves must work, no matter how pro-poor some of them may be? The answer is a definite yes. It is another matter that the notebooks which civil service aspirants are systematically made to memorize in the coaching institutes (and elsewhere) in order to succeed in the exam will not help them to succeed in seeing the point of this argument.

The power of civil servants (both power to and power over) is the power of the state. The power of the state is, more or less, the power of dominant classes over subordinate classes, expressed through the mediation of institutions of the state and its various mystifying discourses, including of development, nation, caste, religion, etc. Ultimately, civil servants are the servants of dominant classes. This is no less in countries such as India where the state has a (nominally) democratic form. The situation is acute in India given its specific character of capitalism, massive illiteracy or near-illiteracy, absolute and relative poverty, colonial legacy, complicity of an increasingly compradore-type elite in the imperialist subordination of workers, peasants, etc.

When the state form is democratic in a class-divided society, this produces an interesting ideological context. In this context, political-administrative coercion against, and material neglect of, the interests of the masses are not seen as what they are. Often, they are rather seen as how they appear to be. That is, they are seen merely as wrongful action carried out either by this or that party in furtherance of an incorrect policy, or by this or that civil servant who is misinformed or just dishonest/corrupt. A corollary is that acts of repression and acts of nonfulfilment of human needs by the state (officials) are seen as an anomaly, a mistake, that can be rectified by changing the party in power, or its leadership, or by changing civil servants or by making civil servants listen more to their political masters.[10] Another corollary is that, and this point is moot in the present context, when well-meaning people become civil servants (and there are such people), it is believed that things will be much better. This produces the illusion among young people, especially those coming from relatively underprivileged social contexts and villages that 'I can make a difference'. This perhaps explains why some progressives get interested in being a part of the top-level officialdom. They forget that the state is much less an arena of struggle between the tiny property-owning minority and the majority of the population (workers and small-scale self-employed low-income producers), whose policy is a reflection of the balance of power between the two classes, although the state can within limits, be such an arena of struggle. They forget that the state is the main method through which class struggle is ultimately effected and the majority are kept in check. By occupying the commanding heights of the state, and representing a tiny minority (those who control society's productive resources) civil servants are commanders in the field of class struggle, although they are more or less paid for by the toil of the majority.

Consider the theory of commodity fetishism, which represents an ideological inversion, whereby the relationships between producers assume the form of a relation between the products of people's labour (Marx, 1977). This happens when the definite social relation among producers themselves assumes the fantastic form of a relation between objects. Similarly, what actually is an unequal relation—a relation of exploitation and domination/coercion—between classes, which is enforced by the civil servants of the capitalist state, including those who may mean well, and this unequal relation is mistakenly seen as a mere relation between people, i.e.

between voters/citizens/ clients of specific policy-interventions implemented by civil servants on the one hand and leaders/ civil servants on the other. The latter relation on the surface and the underlying relation, the class relation, both are real. One is more real than another. One represents a state of affairs. Another represents a deeper causal structure of relations. In all societies that are class-divided and where there is social oppression based on caste, gender, etc. through which class relations are reproduced, civil servants and politicians exercise power over ordinary citizens. In poorer countries such as India, there is an excess of this power, given their peculiar social-historical conditions (e.g. backward capitalism; colonial legacy, ordinary citizens' lack of education; widespread poverty, etc.). The fetishism of power that the state represents via the power of civil servants 'cannot be eliminated till the state is directly and socially regulated, in much the same way as commodity fetishism... cannot be removed until labour-power is directly and socially regulated' in the interests of the toiling majority (see Das, 2009).

At the minimum, the practical lesson from the above discussion is this: the masses must demand a thorough democratization of the state. This means that excessive power (in the sense of 'power over') of the civil servants must be stripped. A committee of common citizens (including workers, small-scale producers and intellectuals) must have direct oversight over the activity of the civil servants, including their income and daily interactions with politicians and business people. Post-retirement, they must not be able to work for any profit-seeking private company. If this happens, neither will the craze for civil service exams continue, nor will the business of coaching institutes thrive as much as they do. There will be civil servants but they will be servants of the ordinary people living on a wage/salary, and not of the rich business-people and their political spokes-persons/accomplishes (pro-business politicians). As well, there is a need for promoting a counter-hegemonic education in schools, colleges, universities and technical institutes: masses must be provided education about the entire social-political order, its history based in evidence, about the anti-democratic tendencies within society, and how it can be changed by *aam* (ordinary) citizens. To be a proper civil servant, one has to simply work and think on behalf of and in the interest of the toilers of all genders, religions and castes, who constitute the majority of the nation and who are the masters of the civil servants.

Civil servants are, generally speaking, neither civil nor are they servants of the masses, the majority. When will the transition from the civil servants being the servants of the rich and the powerful to being the servants of the toiling majority happen? When will civil servants be truly civil servants?

## Notes

1. Muslims, lower castes and tribal communities are heavily under-represented.
2. This is not to say that all civil servants all the time behave in this way. It is the case that there have been well-meaning, democratic-minded civil servants (e.g. Mr. Appu, Mr. Bandyopadhyay, Mr. Mander, etc). But we know well how these people are generally dealt with by the system.
3. Many people believe that with the so-called neoliberal turn, the state has less power. This is an utterly mistaken assumption. If the neoliberal state has less power, politicians will not spend millions to get elected in every election since the 1990s, neither will hundreds of thousands of people want to invest so much time and money to become bureaucrats. Nor will there be million-dollar scandals after scandals which signify the looting of public resources in the hands of the clique comprising civil servants as well as political leaders and the business-people.
4. Such a regime is called formal subsumption of labour as a form of capitalist class relation. For details on how to reconceptualize capitalism in general and capitalism in the less developed countries, see: Das (2012d; also Das, 2017a: Chapter 8).
5. This necessarily does not mean that economically advanced societies in the West are paragons of democracy. Democracy is a form of class rule, and class is the most important form of inequality. But between two class societies, the state in one can be somewhat more democratic than another, overall (if not in every respect). In the relatively more advanced societies, one does not see the kind of power relation between the masses (in their everyday life) and the bureaucracy. It is true that along with bureaucracies, there are lobbyists and law-professionals and media houses who perform useful functions for the ruling classes in developed societies, and perhaps, over time in India, many educated

people will perform these roles and may not opt for civil services as much as they do now.

All states, neoliberal or not, will have civil servants. This is true about India and the US. The question is not about the very existence of civil servants. The question is much rather this: why it is that civil servants in countries such as India are the kind of 'semi-kings' that they are? To what extent does this situation reflect a colonial mentality on the part of ordinary citizens and civil servants?

6. There is indeed a direct association between increasing inequality and increasing authoritarianism of the state, in all societies. In post-revolution Russia, when the masses were living in great poverty, 'the bureaucratic caste' was living relatively well. This kind of inequality can only be defended by an authoritarian state. Of course, the rise of an authoritarian tendency cannot be explained entirely in terms of inequality. The civil war, the imperialist encirclement of the new state and other factors contributed to the process. Consider the present-day US: given the massive amount of inequality, which has worsened since the 2008 economic crisis, the state has become increasingly authoritarian.
7. The propertied class and all those with sufficient money can buy a bit of democracy (including rule of law, decent treatment from officials, etc.).
8. Here we should remind ourselves of the point made earlier. Civil servants (and politicians) accept bribes from the business class to make quick money. They help the business class to make quick money. Just imagine how quickly one can make money if with help from civil servants (and politicians), one is just given large tracts of government land for almost nothing.
9. Indeed, this kind of illusion is propagated in the form of social capital and state-society synergy literature in academia (see the work of Peter Evans and the like).
10. In this context, one must be critical of the current euphoria among sections of the middle class for a new party (Aam Aadmi party) which has had some electoral success based on the promise of a more honest government. Corruption indulged in by the civil servants and politicians cannot be separated either from the illegitimate practices on the part of property-owners (e.g. ignoring minimum wage laws or factory safety laws) nor from the overall undemocratic impulses of the state, which, as argued here, are rooted in the definite class character of the society. There are very severe limits indeed to the success of the fight against corruption on the part of any political formation (petty bourgeois or bourgeois), which lacks a proletarian-democratic agenda, which is one of thorough democratization over property as well as the state, and indeed all aspects of life.

# 5

# What Kind of Education for What Kind of Society?

In India, many good students, after completing their tenth grade, spend a lot of their time in coaching classes. Time spent there often comes at the expense of the time that can be spent in colleges/universities. They do this in order to prepare themselves for entrance exams for engineering and medical seats.[1] Even if they do attend colleges/universities full-time, their main aim is to sit for the entrance exams. The coaching institutes which prepare students for the entrance exams are, more or less, in the for-profit sector.[2] And increasingly, engineering and medical students are going to the colleges for their degrees, which are in the for-profit sector. All this is a part of increasing privatization of education in neoliberal India, and raises several questions concerning education and society. These are schematically presented below.

1. Parents pay an excessive amount of money for seats for their children. In many cases, they sell their assets or take loans. They save by reducing their monthly and daily expenditures. And many people make a lot of money out of this education business. But what kind of education in these colleges are their children receiving? Many of the so-called medical and engineering colleges may be ill-equipped to teach the relevant subjects. Many of the private engineering colleges hire teachers who have completed only an undergraduate degree in engineering in other (ill-equipped) private colleges. Have

these teachers had a chance to polish their teaching abilities? Are there proper lab facilities in these colleges?

2. What is the outcome of the current system of technical education in India for the country as a whole? In a country of a billion plus, how many doctors does the system produce who actually invent new ways of curing an illness, as opposed to writing prescriptions on the basis of knowledge produced mainly in the advanced countries? Similarly, how many thousands of engineers do we manufacture who produce knowledge about new ways of making things? More importantly, how many scientists—in biological or natural sciences—do we produce who produce new ways of understanding nature and the human body?

3. Is the craze for professional-technical education promoting an overall scientific culture, a culture that encourages lay-people to be rational and to find empirically verifiable reasons for events around them rather than explain phenomena in terms of these: mystical, unverifiable, imagined things (including imagined things from the past), actions of gods and goddesses and their managers/brokers? Is it at all surprising that in the current atmosphere where rationalism has become the sacrificial cow, many people who believe in irrational ideas appear to have received education in science and technology?

4. The British system produced clerks in India. Is independent India not producing a different kind of 'clerk' or a similar kind of people: sophisticated semi-coolies, tech coolies and the like, out of the population that goes into so-called professional institutions? Is it not interesting that many engineers in India spend their working time reading/processing credit card statements transmitted from the rich countries, which amounts to keeping records? Do they need engineering skills acquired from colleges to perform these tasks? Or, is it that the kind of education they receive makes them suitable for only this kind of semi-skilled, techno-coolie jobs, and nothing better?

5. Arguably, the aim of education, real education, should promote development in two senses: a) self-development (changing ourselves, our ways of thinking, making us more scientific in our attitude and more critical of things happening around us), and b) social development understood as increasing ability to contribute to a democratic, secular, economically advanced and fairer society and to an ecologically sustainable reproduction of natural systems.[3] Now, is being an engineer or a doctor (and in the ways in which people become engineers and doctors) necessarily the main way of achieving real education?

6. One cannot at all deny the importance of forces of technology and medicine. But to what extent is it the case that the major problems of human society can be solved through the actions of engineers and doctors, and the like, who mainly keep recycling old knowledge assembled in big textbooks written in advanced countries, and whose main aim is to make money? What about a scientist who finds new ways in which nature works, and new ways in which nature can be suitably 'modified' in an ecologically sustainable way and in the interest of humanity as a whole rather than in the interest of patent-seeking business people, who have been making an all-out attempt to own/commodify nature and knowledge about nature? What about a scientist who uses her/his scientific knowledge to fight not only irrationalism in culture but also corporates' attempts to own science and nature in the private interest, or who organizes protests against war that destroys ordinary people by using high-tech methods, or who organizes people to fight for better public health? What about a labour lawyer who fights for the rights of workers and poor peasants, or a human rights lawyer who fights for the rights of religious minorities and of women and children, who are increasingly subjected to violence from right-wing forces? What about a professor who aims at changing the collective self-consciousness of a society, who aims at making us rethink the directions in which a society is moving? What about a professional who can organize and manage the cooperatives of poor women or workers' coops? What about a political scientist or a sociologist who can organize, or who can inspire activists

to organize, the poor masses in new ways to help them develop confidence in their ability to change things in the world and to fight for their rights independently of those forces who wish to preserve the current system (in slightly modified ways)? What about the role of socially conscious journalists who consistently and courageously lay bare the criminal conduct and corruption of our economic and political elites? What about artists and storytellers who can feel the pulse of a society and represent it in beautiful ways for us to enjoy and learn from? How about promoting an education system that produces writers/poets like Premchand, Tagore, Shelley, etc.?

7. When parents push their children into narrow technical education and when children opt for that kind of education, sometimes against their own internal desire as movies such as *Three Idiots* portray, do people think about these other options? If not, what stops them from thinking about these options? What is the implication of a society over-emphasizing so-called professional education? Is it not true that in part because of the sort of financial as well as ideological-political emphasis on technical-professional education that we see, other kinds of education (including in basic sciences; social sciences) are neglected?

8. Our ideas about society and ourselves, including what we wish to do in our lives, are not created autonomously in our heads. They are generally shaped by the kind of society we live in, even if we are not fully conscious of this fact. One must ask: why is this kind of education being promoted? What are the forces (i.e. commercial and state-bureaucratic interests) that drive the rush for engineering and medical seats? In more direct ways: to what extent is our obsession with the so-called professional education driven by the fact that investors make money by selling professional education as a commodity and by the fact that this kind of education is making India (and other similar countries) a cheap low-wage platform of global capitalism, both for its own business people and international business? To what extent are our bureaucrats and politicians benefiting from this business directly because they also invest

in this and/or because they enable/allow such investment and thus make money in the process? Is it not the case that by allowing the growth of privatized education system in the form of coaching institutes to prepare students for entrance exams, and indeed similar other forms of privatization of education, the state is absolved of its duty to provide high quality affordable education at all levels, starting with primary and secondary levels? To what extent might it be true that India's technical-professional education-for-profit is creating a 'compradore' educated elite (whether its members work in India or abroad), which acts as a conduit through which the country is subordinated to international business and imperialist states?

9. Therefore, and ironically, is it not the case that: the kind of mind-numbing education that exists is stopping us—or discouraging us—from asking questions that challenge the nature of education that the country is providing, and therefore, the nature of society we live in?

To conclude: It is true that the major problems of India or other countries are not amenable to genuine and long-term solutions at national and global scales through merely scientific and technological fixes in the current society. This is a society where wealth is controlled by a tiny minority and is used to produce more wealth for that minority. Major problems of society do not exist mainly because of the lack of scientific and technological knowledge that would promote more food production. People are not hungry because we do not have enough food. It is simply wrong to say that it is necessary to use science and technology (e.g. the use of genetically modified seeds) to increase food production in order to address hunger.

To say that science and technology hold the key to the solution of major problems—especially, problems of hunger, and lack of healthcare and of housing, etc. for the majority of people—is a type of scientistic and technicistic suggestion that is simply wrong. Yet, scientific and technical education is necessary in every country, including in India. In this context, one may consider the following propositions. a) Scientific and technological knowledge can, within limits, satisfy people's needs (consider tremendous increase in longevity that has been possible in India and elsewhere partly because of such knowledge). b) That such knowledge promotes a rational and scientific culture among ordinary citizens stopping them from falling prey to obscurantism and superstition, a culture that also helps them to understand society and history scientifically (given much common ground between a scientific understanding of nature and that of society). The absence of such a culture and therefore the presence of superstitious ideas that are spreading in India can limit the contribution of technology towards human welfare. c) Scientific and technical knowledge by making productivity increases possible and by promoting a scientific culture can create material and cultural conditions for a future society where such knowledge can be used differently (i.e. to satisfy ordinary people's needs and not to produce profit for a minority). Science and technology education is too important to be left to the profit-seeking private investors and to a culture of coaching institutes which inculcate a method of learning (e.g. rote learning) that is too narrow and, ultimately, unscientific in that it does not promote a desire to be inquisitive.

## Notes

1. It is not clear how someone can learn theory from one set of 'teachers' in coaching classes, and learn about the practical matter (e.g. labouratory work) from certified college/university teachers?
2. That the coaching institutes are becoming big business and that they are a big lobby influencing the quality of education is increasingly clear, including from the incidents of leakage of question papers for the examinations held by boards of education.
3. I am not denying that in the current form of society, education helps one get a job and that getting a job is necessary for one to pay one's bills. There is nothing wrong if one seeks an education partly from the perspective of earning a livelihood.

# 6

# The Hindu Right's Model of Development

During the 2014 general elections, the so-called Gujarat model of development was much discussed. Various criticisms of this model have been raised. These criticisms should not be seen at all as criticisms of Gujarat as a province or of people living there. In fact, what is being claimed as the Gujarat model should be more properly be called the Modi model of development—some appropriately call it the Modani model.[1] This is a state which, like many other states, is rich in natural resources, culture, and human abilities. Like any other place, it has its own problems, the problems which the whole country shares, and indeed, many other parts of the world share. The so-called Gujarat model is a Hindu Right Model of development, which happens to have been implemented by a right-wing party.

The proponents of this model say that Gujarat is the number one state in many respects, that its economic growth rate has been much faster than other states, that it has attracted much foreign investment and has industrialized fast, and so on. Opponents, including supporters and sympathizers of Congress and its allies, say that Gujarat's economic growth rate is not as high as it is said to be, or that Gujarat's human development record is not that good, that inequality is increasing in Gujarat, and so on. Often the debate boils down to this. Some people say that: the Gujarat model of development is the best and it is Modi's model, which should be emulated by all states, and indeed developing countries. Others say that: the Gujarat model is a myth, a big lie, a scam, that there is nothing so special about Gujarat.[2]

Not everything can by a lie. Those who support the model say that in this respect and in that respect, Gujarat under the BJP has done better than other places and that the ways in which the government has done this can be emulated elsewhere. The model includes an empirical fact (i.e. in some respects Gujarat has indeed done well, and this should be acknowledged), and the model has a normative content (that it should be followed by other states).

It is not difficult to refute the exaggerated view that color-paints the claim. It has been refuted by many (Hensman, 2014; Dreze, 2014). It has been established that: Gujarat's economic growth rate is high, but not as high as it is claimed to be. Gujarat's record on wages or on child mortality rates or on literacy is not that good either, relative to many other relatively industrialized and high-income states. Much of what the Modi-ite government has achieved, it has done so by giving away natural resources and government loans at almost zero cost to certain business groups who have also received huge tax concessions, all of which could have been used to benefit the common people.

In terms of single indicators of development (wages, literacy, per capita income, sex ratio, etc.), Gujarat is nowhere near or at the top.[3] The average urban daily wage for casual workers in Gujarat is Rs. 106. The All India urban average for casual labour is Rs. 121. More developed states such as Punjab (Rs. 136), Andhra Pradesh (Rs. 138) and Kerala (Rs. 216) are way ahead of Gujarat in terms of how they treat their working population. What is worse, the urban daily wage for casual labour in poorer states like Rajasthan (142) and Uttarakhand (Rs. 136) is also above Gujarat while bimaaru Bihar is on par at Rs. 105. Rural Gujarat fares no better. The average casual rural wage in Gujarat is Rs. 83 per day. The All India average is Rs. 93. Even so called bimaaru Bihar fares far better at Rs. 114—almost 40 per cent better (*Times of India* January 1,

2013). An average rural worker in the organized sector in Gujarat gets Rs. 254 per day as against a National average of Rs. 298, with bimaaru Bihar yet again outstripping Gujarat at Rs. 412. And the story of urban Gujarat is the worst of the lot. An urban organized sector worker in Gujarat makes Rs. 320 per day as against a national average of Rs. 450 and bimaaru Bihar at Rs. 412. In short, amongst organized sector urban workers, Gujarat is 40 per cent below the national average and nearly 30 per cent below Bihar (*Times of India* January 1, 2013).

The infant mortality rate (IMR)—the number of deaths per 1,000 live births of children under one year of age—is one of the most important indicators of development. Gujarat's IMR is 33 in 2015, and it is higher than IMR in other relatively affluent states like Maharashtra (21) and Punjab (23) and in not-so-affluent states like Himachal Pradesh (28), Jammu and Kashmir (26), Sikkim (18), Nagaland (12) and Tripura (20). Between 2006 and 2015, Gujarat achieved just 37.7 per cent reduction in IMR while the rate of reduction was much higher in affluent states such as Punjab (48 per cent) and Maharashtra (40 per cent) and in not so affluent states such as Jammu and Kashmir (50 per cent), Sikkim (45 per cent), and Himachal (44 per cent) (Mohammad, 2017).

Since much statistical evidence has been provided to refute the exaggerated claim about the Gujarat model, I will only briefly cite some evidence from reports that make use of composite index of development. In terms of Human Development indices, Gujarat had a score of 0.466 in 1999-2000 and 0.527 in 2007-08, while the best ranking state, Kerala, had a score of 0.677 and 0.790. Gujarat is in the middle. In terms of the composite index of environmental sustainability, in 2010, Gujarat, ranked at 23, has one of the lowest scores among all the 28 states, with its score of 20 (on a scale of 0 to 100) (http://www.greenindiastandards.com/). In terms of policy effectiveness (which is based on indicators for law and order, and some economic variables), Gujarat's rank is extremely low (at 16) as well.

According to Raghuram Rajan's report on socio-economic backwardness of Indian states, Gujarat is right in the middle. If the least developed State gets a score of 0.798, and the most developed major State gets 0.095, Gujarat has a score of 0.491. Gujarat is in the category of less developed states, which include Bengal, J&K, Karnataka, Himachal and Andhra Pradesh, which are ruled by both BJP and non-BJP parties/formations.

These and similar statistics do not, of course, reflect on the abilities of ordinary people of Gujarat; in fact, they are known as hardworking and innovative, as people in many other places are. What they point to is a wider pattern of geographically uneven capitalist development in India; in fact, inequalities between Indian states have been increasing under neoliberal capitalism. Such a pattern on geographical inequality reflects the specific ways in which national (and global-level) market mechanisms and national-level public policies interact with state-level factors. The state-level factors include: states' level of development at a given point in time (say, in late 1980s); states' resource base; the nature of states' class relations (distribution of property; strength of different sections of the capitalist class); state governments' policies; states' history and culture; opportunities for, and obstacles to, political movements among the masses for greater social-economic justice in a particular state, and so on. And the statistical evidence points to the fact that Gujarat is clearly not number one, and cannot therefore be a model to be emulated. But the matter does not end there.

## For a More Critical Critique: The Gujarat Model of Development as an Ideology

The Modi-ite discourse on Gujarat model requires a more thoroughgoing critique. The Congressi type—'centrist' or 'liberal'—critique of the model is inadequate (and indeed hypocritical), even if some of this critique is correct. It is not enough to reject the Gujarat model by saying that the state is doing worse than other states in this or that respect, or that another model (e.g. Tamil Nadu or Sikkim model) may be better than the Gujarat model. To say that another state such as Tamil Nadu, is doing better than Gujarat, and that therefore there is no such thing as the Gujarat model actually amounts to support for the neoliberal model, because in states like Tamil Nadu both the ruling parties' economic policy is rightwing, almost like BJP's. The rejection of the Gujarat model has to be a part of the rejection of the whole neoliberal-bourgeois model which has been bought in, and accepted, by many critics of the Gujarat model themselves. These critics include, most prominently, the supporters of the entire Congress ideological-political apparatus.

Besides, one must indeed not see the so-called Gujarat model merely as an economic development model. Paraphrasing the superb writing of Terry Eagleton (1991) on ideology, I will say that the Gujarat economic development model is partly an ideology. It is an ideology in that: it is a system of ideas, which are partly false, distorted/deceptive/illusory and partly not so, which are partly empirical and partly not so (i.e. normative); and these ideas are used to create and/or justify polarization. The polarization in question is not only between the vast majority of people struggling to eke out a living and the tiny minority which control's society's resources and governmental power, but also between the religious-majority and religious-minority. The Gujarat model as an ideology is sought to be presented as a hegemonic project as well in the Gramscian sense: it will give some concessions to the economically and socially marginalized (including even to religious minorities), for that is exactly how it seeks to produce consent to the polarizing order. Therefore, the model cannot be merely a *maha jhoot* (a big lie), or merely a massive myth, as some describe it. It cannot merely be a toffee model (giving away things to business for free); it has a wider agenda.

Since the model is constructed to have an ideological effect and to produce consent to the underlying economic-political agenda, it will say x and deliberately not say its opposite, y. By being partial, it can act like a complete whole. Let me give some examples. The model will highlight some achievements (e.g. infrastructural development in rural areas, which has indeed happened under Modi)[4] and exclude its failures (it will not say anything about farmers' suicides or relatively high maternal mortality). It will emphasize certain aspects of the present, and erase the past: Gujarat's development is due to Modi's policies, but apparently it has nothing to do with the fact that Gujarat achieved many things under the (Congress) regimes before Modi. It will say that Gujarat's development is more due to naked neoliberal free-market policies but it will not emphasize the government's ability to provide social services (however limited this may be due to the prevailing balance of power between the rich and the poor). The model will stress that Gujarat is the most economically free state (read: freedom of business-houses). But it will not say that intellectual and political freedom is suppressed by the apparatus of the Right, an apparatus within which there is a well-planned division of labour among its ideological, political, coercive elements. The model will say that it is one of the best-governed states, or perhaps the best,[5] but will not talk about the corruption scandals involving the cosy relations between the government and big business and the fact that religious minorities do not have the freedom to live in peace and without fear or that workers' democratic right to strike is regularly suppressed.

The question is: why is this ideology believed in by people? Why do people believe the man behind the model, who, as Ashish Nandy has said, exhibits a distinctly authoritarian style of functioning, the man who has been described by the American, David Cohen, as India's Reagan?[6] There are many reasons why the Right ideology of development is accepted as widely as it is. There are, of course, processes, rooted in our social structures, which explain why people believe that their everyday problems of income, employment and democratic rights can be resolved by religious beliefs and by religious politics, the politics of hatred against fellow citizens who may be different merely on the basis of religion. This is a vast topic, and will not be discussed here. A more proximate reason for the acceptance of the Right ideology that will be stressed here is this: there are sections of society (often urban, middle class and upper caste people) who are partly products of the post-

1991 new economic policy and who have accepted another ideology, an ideology based on fetishization of commodities, of material things. They 'believe' that one must just expand one's command over money and consumer commodities to lead a good life at any cost, even if the prevailing political regime slaughters/terrorizes fellow citizens, even if it ensures super-exploitation of (fellow) workers, oversees the destruction of the environment and surrenders to a small economic elite the things (e.g. government assets, government land) that belong to society, all in the name of economic development.

Of course, the kind of social arrangements that exist underlie this kind of belief, so it is not a cognitive fault. The Right is making political use of such a belief. The development talk that Modi and the Right engage in is a way to sell the wine of naked neoliberalism in the bottle of development and good governance, and thus to gain power at the Centre,[7] which can be further used to advance the fascistic-communal agenda it has been pursuing for decades under the guidance of a Hindu-supremacist paramilitary organization that has been banned by the Indian government three times. In selling the conservative development ideology to the people, the Right movement and Modi Inc. are being properly helped by the national and global business class (including in the diasporic capitalist and middle class elements) who hope to benefit from a national-level conservative and authoritarian government which will make people gulp bitter pills (read: labour reforms, further privatization of state-owned companies, and the like). The apparatus of the Right often swears by the idea of the nation. But it spends millions of rupees on a foreign firm to sell its ideas to people, and it would indeed do everything possible to further subordinate India's economy and polity (i.e. the economic-political conditions under which the majority live and work) to imperialist companies and governments. That does not mean the right will abandon pursuing the idea of nation in a politically conservative manner: it will extract sacrifices from ordinary people (the actual nation) in the name of the Right's socially-constructed nation,[8] to pursue its bourgeois-communal agenda and to benefit its business clientele.

So it is not enough to say that things have not become significantly better under the Modani model in Gujarat (in some cases, things have improved and in other cases they have not). But the important question is this: even if poverty has come down significantly, even if everyone is able to earn a little more under a regime of the Right and even if there are a few more roads than before, would one prefer a regime that can not only crush the most fundamental freedoms, but also put more and more resources and fruits of labour of ordinary people right into the pockets of big business? Can the Right's promise of better economic performance and governance be detached from its reactionary economic and social-political ideology? Once again a merely empirical and statistical refutation of the Right's model is not enough at all.

## The Congress and the Gujarat Model: More Than Family Resemblances

Ludwig Wittgenstein (2001/1953) talks about family resemblances: this is the idea that things which may appear to be—or thought to be—connected by one essential common feature may indeed be inter-linked by many overlapping similarities, where no one feature is common to all, where there is no underlying essence. Of course, the idea that there is an essence underlying different things/forms is being rejected by postmodernists. It should not be. Are BJP and Congress models mere family resemblances? I fear not. Let me explain.

Criticisms of the Gujarat model from Congress (from the so-called Centre) and its political and intellectual supporters are inadequate. If allowing business people to make money at any cost (with a few crumbs thrown at the poor at one's whim) is the main model of development, Mr. Modi did not introduce that model. The Congress did. The Modi-ite regime has been just shoe-polishing the model slightly, to make the India of the big business shine a bit more. The culture of promoting animal spirits is something the former Prime Minister of India, one who belongs to the top echelons of Congress, and who was the architect of pro-business interventions (euphemistically called reforms), has constantly talked about. In terms of this culture, Congress and BJP have the same essence. They are more or less two cheeks of the same face: if one cheek gets a slap, the other cheek will be available for another. They do not just share some phenomenal, contingent, similarities. Their quarrel is over who will have access to governmental power, which can then be used to promote the same essence, the same agenda: the big business agenda. One (e.g. Congress) might throw a few more dry crumbs down the throats of the poor than another. Their quarrel is not really 'ideological' or one based on principles, as far as economic policy is concerned. The idea that Congress supports progressive capitalists and the BJP supports crony capitalists (this distinction was made in a recent Rahul Gandhi interview) reminds one of the decade-old distinction between compradore and feudal elements in the ruling class on the one hand, and progressive-national bourgeoisie on the other. Both the distinctions are, more or less, as useless as putrid water. It is also the case that if the Right can now make a claim to the state's executive power via the ideology of development (with the kind of force it does now), it is enormously due to the Congress's failure to significantly benefit the masses and reign in corruption during its rule. Its failure is written in the very structure of the organization as the traditional party of the big bourgeoisie and large landowners.[9] Of course, the additional factor, and a very important factor, has been the situation where there is an absence of a credible coherent alternative to BJP and Congress from the standpoint of the masses. Their independent political-ideological mobilization has not occurred, as their political energy has been more or less channelized to narrow electoralism and opportunism by (most segments of) the Left. The Left has more or less opted for a social-democratic vision of development (at least in its official discourse), and it has, in practice, implemented neoliberalism while in power at the provincial level and has supported the central government's pursuing neoliberal-bourgeois agenda. The masses therefore suffer both due to neoliberal capitalism practised by the two major parties of big business, and the ideas/actions of their own leaders (i.e. Left leaders). And in terms of even communalism, it must be said that Congress does not, and will not, stop adapting to, and compromising on, that agenda: one must continue to ask (while refraining from saying Congress is as communal as BJP): why did Congress not stop the 1992 demolition of the Babri mosque or the 1984 massacre of innocent Sikhs? In the latter context, the Cobrapost sting operation sheds some interesting light on the claim of Congress to be secular and to differentiate itself from the Right. And the underlying fact here is that the business class—whose own agenda both the parties seek to enthusiastically put into effect—increasingly pays scant attention to democratic rights and secularism. Money-making is far more important than these lofty ideals.

The discussion on the Gujarat model represents a process of differentiation of the neoliberal paradigm which both parties and their spokespersons advocate for: the Right just signifying a more naked form of neoliberalism and a blatantly non-secular view than Congress.[10] The progressives' critique of the development model that both Congress and BJP have been promoting has become, more or less, a critique of merely neoliberalism (a conjunctural form of capitalism), and additionally, the critique of neoliberalism, in some circles, has become merely a critique of an extreme form of neoliberalism, one that is propagated by the Right. Such a process of discursive differentiation has been somewhat successful in blunting the edge of the real critique of the economic-political conditions in which the vast majority live. So what could be a serious critique of the system has been dumbed down and muted at two levels. There is indeed a real danger to some people (e.g. Zoya Hasan, 2014) carelessly describing Congress' policies as social democratic, suggesting that as a party, in its current form, it is a progressive alternative, in itself, to the Right. It is not, as far as economic policy is concerned.[11] Some people call Congress socialist or associate it with socialism. Such views on Congress are simply false views. The criticism of BJP and Congress models of development must be from one single (=common) standpoint. This is the standpoint of the majority of people who have to work for a wage and/or are petty (commodity) producers and are barely living a human life.

The criticism of the model must be from the standpoint of the necessity for toiling people to have significant democratic control over society's resources and government policy, and from the standpoint which preserves the democratic rights of all genders, castes and religious groups. The Gujarat model of development—and indeed the broader neoliberal model itself which Congress embraces—negates all these standpoints. The following should be repeated: not only has the Gujarat government turned over society's resources (land, ports, public sector loans) to the big business. Any democratic opposition to it is also often suppressed. Is it not important that Gujarat accounts for 5 per cent of India's population, but it accounts for more than 20 per cent of murders and assaults of Right to Information activists, who play an important democratic role in society?

To say that the Gujarat model is faulty on the ground that it may have promoted growth but it has not promoted human development is necessary but not adequate. This is because such a criticism accepts that satisfying interests of business houses which is allowed to drive economic growth, on the one hand, and satisfying ordinary people's economic and cultural needs, on the other, are both possible within the neoliberal-capitalist model. This is a model that is supported by the Right movement as well as by most of the critics of the movement. These critics include people from the Congress and its various regional variants and opportunistic avatars and other regional implementers of the neoliberal order. They believe that the neoliberal model—letting a society and its economy be run by the animal spirits of profit-making in the hands of (large-scale) private capitalists—is basically correct except that the government needs to spend a few more rupees per person on education, health, etc., (as Amartya Sen and the like suggest), and perhaps preferably in a decentralized manner (i.e. at the state and district levels), so that ordinary working people can be under the juggernauts of the entire conservative economic model in a somewhat more consenting and capable manner. On the surface they are critics of the Modani model. But by accepting the neoliberal model itself of which the Modani model is just an expression, they are actually much less critical of it than they think. Such criticisms and associated political practice can neither achieve development with a human face nor stop fascistic tendencies. Intellectually and politically, the critique of the Right must be from a standpoint which is critical of both the Right and Modinomics and its 'liberal' type critics such as Amartya Sen (see Das, 2001a). In fact, Modinomics, Manmohanomics and Seninomics are, more or less, members of a family, a family within which there is considerable dissent but one that does not go beyond a given boundary.[12] There are more quantitative differences among them than qualitative differences. All are forms of bourgeois thinking and of interventions that ultimately serve bourgeois interests.

Some say that it is wrong to equate the economic policies of the Congress and the BJP because unlike in the case of Congress, the most distinguishing feature of the Right's agenda is that Hindu assertion is considered to be a prerequisite for economic growth and prosperity. This view is partly mistaken. Let us assume, only for the sake of an argument, that BJP is actually interested in the welfare of Hindus. Given that Hindus are the majority of ordinary citizens, should we not expect that at least they would have a decent life relative to the super-rich that Modi and the Right work for?[13] Gujarat's workers, Hindus or not, are paid one of the lowest wage-rates in India. Besides, and importantly, BJP or its business supporters cannot live on Hinduism or in temples, although Hindutva[14] is a part of its overall agenda. The socio-economic system—and especially when it is in a political-economic crisis[15]—must divide the ordinary people and weaken their opposition to immiserization, inequality and oppression. This division happens on the basis of religion (and other social identities). The Right happens to provide the ideas and ideological resources such as religion (and sometimes location, as well as in the case of the Shiv Sena, and so on). In the process, the Right satisfies illusory interests of some people (especially petty bourgeois people and possibly lumpen elements in the working class). For Hindus of both types (those who believe that religion and politics should be kept separate, and those who believe in communal politics), worshipping Hindu gods and goddesses is an important part of life. They believe that gods and goddesses can be of help in times of need. For them a need for religion is a real need.[16] As long as religious beliefs and religious practice act as a coping mechanism in a society that is full of suffering and oppression, and is a force for some kind of harmony, and is, more or less, a private affair in which the state is not involved, religion is relatively less of a problem. But the problem arises when religion is made use of for political gains.

The political mobilization of religious sentiments by conservative Hindutva forces seeks to make some people think that gods and goddesses are/were actually real beings, that they have/had a place in the world, and are associated materially with a temple here or a setu there, and that those places need to be defended against the encroachment by non-Hindus, which has caused religious suffering for Hindus, etc. It is only a short step from the above scenario to this following: questions of mandirs and setus—questions of the non-satisfaction of religious needs and questions of religious suffering—become more important than questions of non-satisfaction of material needs, such as need for food, shelter, education and healthcare, etc. As well, political mobilization on the basis of religion produces a psychological compensation to lower-income Hindus, those who are actually suffering in material terms, for they come to identify themselves with upper-caste and wealthier Hindus, including Hindu business people, on the basis of a homogenized Hindu identity. The fact that the poor and rich Hindus are a part of the same group, same Hindu nation, is a source of psychological satisfaction. So Hindu workers and peasants who should be fighting the exploitative property-owners who also happen to be Hindus tend to identify with these property-owners. Such a process produces the following dual result: class opposition of exploited, poor Hindus to property-owning, rich Hindus is replaced with class-collabouration between them on the basis of common religious identity, while animosity is created between, say, Hindu workers/citizens and non-Hindu workers/citizens, when in fact there should be class-political unity between them. The objective impact of Hindutva politics and thinking is exactly this: the reproduction of an exploitative class system that oppresses the majority and stuffs the pockets of a minority.

The Modi model is Moditva (Nandy, 2010), a combination of rabid communalism and naked neoliberalism, one in which neoliberal-bourgeois politics is the dominant aspect (Das, 2010). In this model, even slaughter of cows is to be prohibited, but the slaughter of living human beings if they belong to a particular religion can very well be encouraged and the fact that millions of human beings die untimely deaths due to lack of food and medicine, etc. or that millions are malnourished can be well tolerated. In this model, profit of the business people, whether Hindus or not, comes far ahead of ordinary people, whether Hindus or not. To generalize what is happening: things (money, consumer items, roads, electricity), as in neoliberal culture, and certain animals, artifacts and myths, as in reactionary religious imagination, have more value than human beings.

Common to both Congress and BJP type of thinking and to any variations of them is this: worshipping of money, the mania of money, the fetish of money. If one has money, even without much education, one can be a great orator, by just hiring speech writers and media spin-machines. If you have no power to convince people to vote for you or if your policies are anti-people, but if you have money, you can win elections by spending millions to make people believe in your ideas and to bribe poverty-stricken voters. If you have money, you can use it to destroy huge historical monuments and make a mockery of democratic principles, within a few hours. If you are a criminal who is directly responsible for, or who is complicit in, the killing of innocent men, women and children, you can call yourself innocent and you can get people to declare you are innocent, by using money to hire the smartest lawyers and by bribing or threatening anyone who might say anything against you. If you have money, you can bribe enough number of politicians to get certain legislations passed even if these are against the interests of the masses and even if these merely satisfy the interests of imperialist businesses, imperialist governments and the domestic big business.

One is reminded of the following lines, written more than 150 years ago by Marx on 'The Power of Money' (1844):

The extent of the power of money is the extent of my power. Money's properties are my—the possessor's—properties and essential powers. Thus, what I am and am capable of is by no means determined by my individuality.

'I am ugly, but I can buy for myself the most beautiful of women. Therefore I am not ugly, for the effect of ugliness—its deterrent power—is nullified by money. I, according to my individual characteristics, am lame, but money furnishes me with twenty-four feet. Therefore I am not lame.

I am bad, dishonest, unscrupulous, stupid; but money is honoured, and hence its possessor. Money is the supreme good, therefore its possessor is good. Money, besides, saves me the trouble of being dishonest: I am therefore presumed honest. I am brainless, but money is the real brain of all things and how then should its possessor be brainless?

Besides, he can buy clever people for himself, and is he who has... power over the clever not more clever than the clever? Do not I, who thanks to money am capable of all that the human heart longs for, possess all human capacities? Does not my money, therefore, transform all my incapacities into their contrary?....

If I have no money for travel, I have no need—that is, no real and realizable need—to travel. If I have the/vocation/for study but no money for it, I have no vocation for study—that is, no/effective/, no/true/vocation. On the other hand, if I have really/no/vocation for study but have the will and the money for it, I have an/effective/vocation for it.'

## Notes

1. This refers to the close interaction between Mr. Modi's regime and the Adani group of industries who have benefited enormously from the regime in the form of cheap land, etc. This also refers to a neoliberal-communal mode of development.

2. While implementing the Gujarat model, Mr. Modi's regime gave Tata Rs. 30,0000 millions, including 1,100 acres land, and against a Tata investment in the small car project of 20,000 million rupees, an interest free loan from the Gujarat Government worth Rs. 95,700 million. Bribe, or welfare for big business? Any of these names would do.
3. However, to say that this fact necessarily signifies a failure of the right-wing model of the Modi-ite regime is faulty because this fact (i.e. the failure of Gujarat to be at the top) must be also seen in terms of what was happening before this regime (i.e. during the Congress regime), just as attributing whatever success the state has achieved to the Modi-ite regime is faulty, on the same ground (i.e. a part of the current level of its development must have its origin in the pre-Modi times).
4. One can say that there are potholes on many roads in Gujarat and therefore there is nothing like Gujarat model is also not adequate: there are such potholes in every state. There are also potholes on the city roads in Toronto and in Detroit, but that will not deter people from saying that Canada and the US are economically advanced countries, and many people in the world would like to follow their models of development.
5. The 'best governed', more or less, means that the government bends the rule to allow the big business to make as much money as it can and thus make the best use of the natural resources and of ordinary people's lives in its own interest.
6. It may be recalled, Reagan, along with Britain's Thatcher, 'inaugurated' neoliberalism in the Western world, in part by politically crushing the bargaining power of ordinary toiling people.
7. The BJP actually won power at the Centre after this article was written.
8. A further discussion on this theme is in the next Chapter.
9. This is the case even if this is also true that there are people in it who have somewhat social democratic and progressive inclinations. But then individual outliers do not define the central tendency of an organization. As a party of the big business, Congress, that obedient instrument of bourgeois-nationalist opposition against imperialism, must do what the big bourgeoisie needs it to do. During its relatively weaker moments, between the 1940s and 1980s, this class benefited enormously from Congress that used state power to lay common conditions for bourgeois development. Congress cannot abandon its function for its economic masters. If BJP uses religion, nation and vikas as ideological tools to mobilize support for its bourgeois policies, Congress has used its own ideological tools—its version of secularism and development, and the history of its involvement in the nationalist movement—with which to mobilize support for its bourgeois policies. The difference between the two had dramatically diminished since the 1990s when neoliberal capitalism under Congress' tutelage began its debut.

10. Once again, more or less, it is the case that BJP is Right Congress, to the extent that one can make any differentiation between the two.
11. This does not necessarily mean, to repeat, that within it there are not people with social-democratic instincts.
12. All of them support private property and market economics. Sen (2000) says: 'What is needed is not a rejection of the positive role of the market mechanism in generating income and wealth…'. In his address to the UN General Assembly, Sen (2004) said: 'The central question is not—indeed cannot be— whether or not to use the market economy. That shallow question is easy to answer, since it is impossible to achieve much economic prosperity without making extensive use of the opportunities of exchange and specialization that market relations offer. Even though the operation of the market economy can be significantly defective (for example because of asymmetric—and more generally imperfect—information), which must be taken into account in making public policy, nevertheless there is no way of dispensing with the institution of markets in general as an engine of economic progress'. If asking whether markets should be used is a shallow question, one should also ask whether the following questions are shallow questions: can one consider the virtues of the market in abstraction from the issue of who (private capitalists or groups of people who perform work and who have no private ownership) controls the commodities and their production; or, more specifically, is the market in which the Tatas, the Birlas, the Adanis, the Toyotas, the Googles, operate the same market as the market in which women street hawkers, indigenous communities selling tendu leaves, self-employed Muslim weavers and worker coops, operate?; and, can one consider the virtues of the market in abstract from the question of to what extent and whether governments can control markets significantly in the interests of the bottom 70-80 per cent, and why exactly has this control not happened which is why we have been experiencing one global crisis after another and which is why income and wealth inequality has been increasing in ways that are unheard of?
13. Consider the conditions of Patidars and their anger against the Modi-ite regime.
14. Associated with this is the idea of India as a place of, and for, Hindus, and where non-Hindus and those Hindus who do not fall in line with the Hindus proper (mainly the higher castes) should remain subordinated to Hindus' culture or to whatever Hindus decide to be their (the Indian) way of life.
15. This is when there is relative economic stagnation in the system (in terms of the absence of long-term increase in income and productivity), when the system blatantly fails to satisfy people's material and social needs (need for food, shelter, education, healthcare, etc.) and therefore when it is difficult to control the anger of the masses, which develops

in a molecular way, and sometimes, erupts openly and without giving prior notice to the headquarters of the political parties that are in charge of politically managing the system that is failing.

16. Belief in religious ideas, however irrational it may seem, it is 'the expression of real suffering and a protest against real suffering. Religion is the sigh of the oppressed creature, the heart of a heartless world, and the soul of soulless conditions. It is the opium of the people' (Marx, 1843).

# 7

# The Hindu Right's Nationalist Worldview and Democracy in India

It is not just that India has become a country where the fetish of money or the mania for money has become very strong. Something else has been happening in tandem.

Today's India has also become a country where it is increasingly not likely that 'the mind is without fear and the head is held high'. It is a country where the mind is not 'led forward into ever-widening thought and action'. It is a place where knowledge is not free, and where words do not 'come out from the depth of truth'. And all this is happening due to the self-appointed knowledge-police, which knows all about the history of India and its culture, and for which Indian history and culture associated with non-Hindus are of little value, whereas all things Hindu are of supreme significance. India has become a country where 'the clear stream of reason' has indeed 'lost its way into the dreary desert sand of dead habit'. The country is being 'broken up into fragments by narrow domestic walls', constructed with the cement of loyalty to religious prejudice, in spite of the fact that it has had a proud argumentative history of religious tolerance (Sen, 2005) and in spite of the fact that lofty spiritual values have been recorded in ancient texts associated with different religious traditions (Hinduism, Islam, Buddhism, Christianity, etc.), which utopian as they may be, reflect humanity's need for harmony with one another and inside one's own self, among other things.[1]

Events at the prestigious Universities (e.g. Jawaharlal Nehru University, and Hyderabad Central University) which symbolize the ongoing attack on democracy and secularism in India are widely known, so I will not narrate these here. What has happened there is a part of the ongoing campaign of the saffron family—a group of communalist-fascistic political and semi-political organizations with the support of formal political parties such as the BJP—is to convert India into a Hindu nation on the basis of cultural nationalism. In its view: Muslims and Christians—and Marxists/communists—are all outsiders. It is interesting that 'Communists and Jihadists at Work in JNU' is the title of a pamphlet authored by the BJP leader Mr. Punj. The right-wing government is placing fascistic Hindu nationalist ideologues in charge of the universities and cultural institutions. It is working with the ABVP, the student wing of the RSS, to target secular-democratic opponents of the saffron family among university students and teachers.

Large sections of the police and judiciary are also openly supporting the government campaign. Justice Rani who heard the bail plea of Kanhaiya Kumar, the JNU's Student Union President, said this, "The thoughts reflected in the slogans raised' [at the JNU rally[2]] cannot be claimed to be protected as the fundamental right to freedom of speech and expression." Such thoughts are an "infection which needs to be controlled/cured before it becomes an epidemic." And "If the infection results in infecting the limb to the extent that it becomes gangrene, amputation is the only treatment.". Clearly communal-fascistic ideas have infected parts of the judiciary.

## Nationalism of the Right-Wing Movement

There are at least three views of what nation means. The saffron idea of nation is the one which treats the nation as devoid of classes, and which, even worse, treats the nation in religious terms as in the Hindu nation, one that is homogeneous and is above any economic or class distinctions. In his 'Introduction' to *Bunch of Thoughts*, a manifesto of saffronism, Prof. Venkat Rao writes: "Another advantage of the Indian [read RSS] view of society is that it eschews class war. It postulates social harmony... The state is not a class agent of the upper class. Nor is it an exploiting agency. It is an agent of morality or dharma". (pp. xxxii—xxxiii) (Quoted in Chattopadhyay, 2014).

This view must be completely rejected. And associated with this view is the very notion of 'anti-national' statements constituting a crime/sedition, and this view is deeply undemocratic and must be rejected as well. Dissent—right of religious and other minorities to have a different opinion than the majority—is an inherent part of democracy. Any force that suppresses dissent in the name of national unity or national development or in the name of protecting a homogenized culture[3] is clearly indicating that, for example, the Hindutva nationalist forces are under threat and cannot win arguments in democratically conducted debates. These elements, who are self-appointed defenders of the Hindu religion, seek to rule by coercion.[4] It is an attack on free speech that is traceable to colonial times.

The view of democracy that flows from, and is associated with this view of nationalism, is also reactionary: if the majority are defined on the basis of religious identity, if the Hindus are the majority, the government of the country will forever be in the hands of that religious group. Such a view of nationalism and democracy is based on the imagined idea that all Hindus have suffered at the hands of all non-Hindus (especially, Muslims). It also assumes that the definition of a social group based on their religious beliefs, which are beliefs that cannot be scientifically backed up, is a valid category for civil, scientific and politically defensible thinking about society. Such a view basically promotes a type of thinking according to which problems of a country can be seen in terms of the divide between a population that practises Hindu religion and one that practises other religions, and that explains problems in terms of rising numerical (or other form of) importance of the non-Hindu population. This is a form of communal Malthusianism.

Secondly, there is the imperialized nation vis-a-vis imperialist nation, and the associated right to self-determination of the oppressed nation. And, nowadays, this means self-determination in relation to imperialist capital and imperialist institutions such as the World Bank. One can defend this view. The capitalist saffron family will not defend this view, in any consistent, principled manner. In fact, the saffron government has just surrendered the nation's sovereignty by the logistics agreements whereby India has become effectively a military base for the supreme imperialist power on earth that has launched an endless series of wars against poorer nations.[5]

Then there is the nation of exploited classes: workers and poor peasants who constitute the majority of the nation on the basis of scientific criterion, i.e. social-economic basis (class relations), vis-a-vis the exploiting classes, who are a small minority. The aim of the saffron family is to promote non-class based politics, a politics based on religious divide. The aim of class politics that the saffron family rejects is to help the nation of workers and peasants to 'rise to be the leading class of the nation', although 'not in the bourgeois sense of the word'.[6] In this view, nationalism means, above anything else, respect for democratic and economic rights of the majority, the toilers.[7] If a toiling family of 3 needs at least Rs. 20,000 a month to live, the BJP government, like that of Congress, will not raise the minimum wages beyond Rs. 7,000. Not respecting this view of the nation, i.e. the nation of toilers, is to, as Tagore would say in *Gitanjali*, 'disown the poor' or 'bend [one's] knees before insolent might' (Tagore, 2015: 36). The saffron movement will not accept this view of the nation, the nation as the nation of the poor, the toilers. For it is more important to protect animals (cows) than to protect millions of human beings, living in cramped conditions, experiencing hunger, and malnutrition, and dying an untimely death. It is indeed commendable to check cruelty against animals, and not just cows, but the poor people might say this to those who want to protect cows:

> You may be a model citizen, perhaps a member of the Society for the Prevention of Cruelty to [cows]...; but the thing that you represent [or more accurately, the thing represented by the economic forces whom you ultimately support and

> represent, I mean the capitalists, the moneybags] face to face with me has no heart in its breast. [The moneybags are there to make money and you are there to create conditions for this to happen by dividing the mass of toilers such as myself]. That which seems to throb there is my own heart-beating. I demand [some food, a nice shelter, a normal working-day, a living wage, good quality healthcare, etc]. [I understand you are concerned about the cruelty to cows, but I am more worried about the cruelty inflicted on me and people like me, by your cow vigilante type actions and the actions of the moneybags whose interests your actions objectively support].
>
> Adapted from Marx's *Capital* (Marx, 1977) (lines in brackets have been added to Marx's lines).

## What Appears to be True is Not True: Hindu Right's Wrong Economic Thinking

The right-wing attack on democracy is not just an attack on democratic rights but is also a class war, a war which is cloaked under the rhetoric and practice of its reactionary view of nationalism and the nation. What the saffron family is doing appears to be just an attack on democracy, including religious freedom, and it appears to belong to the realm of politics. This appearance is only partly true.

Why partly? The RSS/BJP cannot live merely on politics, including its politics of communal violence, fear, and hatred. Nor can it merely thrive on the blessings from gods and goddesses, or exist with the help of the Godses ever-willing to hurt so-called anti-nationals (note Nathuram Godse who was associated with the RSS, and was a devout Brahmin, killed Mohandas K. Gandhi, the Gandhi who led the nationalist movement against the British rule). Nor can the saffron movement just bask in the support from the holy men and holy women peddling its politically-motivated views of Vedic science and the like.[8] The saffron politics is about profane class matters.

The BJP government is openly a pro-market, pro-business, pro-rich, and pro-imperialist government. As an organization that is virtually and for all practical purposes, the right-wing cousin of the Congress Party, the BJP, like Congress, has been implementing right-wing policies (through ordinances).

On March 19, 2016, the national executive of the BJP met and stressed two goals. One was nationalism. The other was: development (read: neoliberal-capitalist development with the state bribing big business, and ignoring working class interests and suppressing its right to organize). Mr. Modi,[9] said this: the issues raised by the opposition—concerning communalism, etc.—are useless issues.

The agenda of the right-wing government is: the intensification of neoliberal pro-capitalist "reform", including reforms to allow easy hire and fire of labour, in order to further strengthen India as a low-wage platform of global capitalism. Its agenda is also the pursuit of the Indian bourgeoisie's great power ambitions through the rapid expansion of India's military, and the harnessing of India to US imperialism's anti-China "pivot." This agenda is implemented by dividing the masses, by injecting fear in them, by suppressing dissent. Religious politics is, dominantly if not entirely, a means of implementing this agenda.

Of course, the ideologues of the saffron movement will deny that they are launching a class war; they will say that they champion the rights of the poor. And some of them do this as individuals.[10] Engaging in a class war is not an individual project. It is a collective project. That is what the saffron movement is fundamentally, if not entirely, about. Every act of the denial of class and class war is a class war. By using the discourse of religion and nation, the saffron family including the fascistic state helps the ruling class to treat some people as subhuman (as second class citizens—people who have less than one unit of citizenship) and therefore worthy of super-exploitation (i.e. as people who can be paid a below average wage). This policy contributed to poverty and other problems, and protects the interests of monopoly businesses, domestic and foreign, who are experiencing problems with profitability. This state (or rather the bloc of political forces controlling it) divides and weakens the mass of working people along religious lines, who would otherwise struggle against these social problems that they experience. When scarcity (of jobs and government benefits) is produced by a capitalist class system, the consequent tension can be released by finding an external enemy: blame is placed by the dominant groups (e.g. middle class Hindus) on, say, religious, ethnic and caste-based minorities.

Large sections of the big business are in an alliance with, and support, these ultra-conservative, fascistic elements, directly or indirectly. After all, they are the ones who would benefit from a 'united' country and not a country where the working masses rise against them. Consider this: In response to the strike of February 2013, the Associated Chambers of Commerce and Industry (Assocham, 2013), said: 'Against its initial estimates of Rs. 15,000-20,000 crore, the GDP may be eroded by about Rs. 26,000 crore, it is apprehended based on the damaging effect of the Bandh on the industrial activity and the services sector like banking, finance' .

The fascistic view of Indian society paints all problems orange or khaki. In this view, what is a conflict between classes is fetishistically seen as a conflict between groups defined in culturalist—religious—terms. In this view, the capitalist class is not the problem. Muslims and Christians are. Or another country—e.g. Pakistan—is. The crushing of dissent—dissent against encroachment on peasants' land, super-exploitation via non-payment of a decent wage, privatization of government enterprises, etc.—is a part of the bourgeois agenda. It is therefore the saffron agenda as well. The saffron agenda is written in letters of blood and fire—in red and orange colours—is a bourgeois agenda. It is not just a cultural and political agenda, although it appears to be so.[11]

Taking advantage of the weakness of the political movement of strata that are committed to democracy, and especially, of the working masses, and of the desperate economic conditions of the masses,[12] the saffron movement is mobilizing petty bourgeois forces (middle class elements, traders, small-scale producers, etc.) by resorting to a combination of multiple things:

demagogy, nationalist rhetoric, some development on the ground, massive lies including history and imagined suffering of Hindus by Muslims, and terror (see Patnaik, 1993; Banaji, 2013). The saffron movement is based on a unified majority based on religion, the idea that the majority are culturally superior and therefore must have political power in its hands. It makes use of massive lies and rumours and resorts to irrational ideas[13] and extermination and/or subjugation of the minorities who do not fall in line.

Inherent in a class society, and in capitalism as a form of class society, there is always an authoritarian tendency: after all the contradiction between formal political equality and actual substantive economic and social inequality remains as does the contradiction between the property-owning class (top 10 per cent or so) and the rest (including the working masses who struggle to eke out a living). Therefore there is always a potential for the masses to rise in rebellion and resist, in covert or overt forms. If some democratic mechanisms and some sort of social harmony (including by bribing minorities with a few concessions) work to reproduce the social order, these are used. Yet, times come when such mechanisms are not helpful. Then masses must be kept in check. They must be stopped from asking for more and for government regulation of businesses and landowners and for welfare interventions, beyond a level the system will tolerate. The need for authoritarianism from the top sometimes even coincides with a felt need for authoritarianism from below (i.e. from petty bourgeois people who are being squeezed). When opportunities for them shrink, they also need an outlet. They need to put the blame on someone, on a group, for a psychological and/or material advantages. The saffron movement is, in many ways, a manifestation of deep authoritarian tendencies that are characteristic a capitalist class-society, although it is not just that. That means that: a fight against the saffron movement is actually a fight for defending democratic rights, which include rights of religious and other minorities, and that such a fight for democracy and secularism must be combined with the fight against the attack on the living standards from the capitalist system, an attack that is aided by the right-wing political forces. It is also clear that such a fight of the masses against the attack on democracy, secularism and living standards, can effectively be launched by the class-forces who create wealth (workers and small-scale producers) for the system in the first place, and who need democracy in order to fight for their social-economic rights. To launch such a fight they must realize that problems of the country such as poverty, low wages and unemployment, and cuts in welfare spending, etc. are not because some people are Hindus and others are not, but because of a capitalist system that is actively supported/managed by the right-wing forces,[14] who are out there to divide the nation on the basis of religion. Because such an action diverts attention of the masses from the root of the problems, the business class also supports the saffron agenda.

The communal politics and thinking such as the one that Hindutva represents, cannot be reduced to the existence of religions. Among other things what the discussion in this and the previous Chapter implicitly or explicitly indicates is that: as long as there are conditions in the world which make people follow a religion, they should have the freedom to do so, that *all* religions contain, however contradictorily and inadequately, some humanistic and lofty ideas about humanity (while they also contain regressive ideas and promote political passivity), that no religious group (the majority or a minority) should suffer from discrimination, that no religion should be seen as inferior or superior to another, that affairs of the state and politics should be kept away from people's religious views/practices (to the maximum extent possible), and that no one should be allowed to politicize people's religiosity and mobilize public support, covertly or overtly, in the name of religion. To the extent that the religious space is important to people to cope with the world they live in, and especially given that religions, including Hinduism, contain progressive and humanistic aspects of life, the *religious space* must not be allowed to be converted into a *communal space*, a space of hatred based on differences between religions. It is perfectly possible for people to be religious and be proud of their religions and not be communal.

It is important that people realize that society's problems such as poverty, unemployment, low wages, etc. do not fundamentally exist because of the religious divide but that when religion-based politics and policies in support of neoliberal capitalism are combined and reinforce each other, problems get worse and economic development gets more lopsided, that the politically-manufactured conflict between religions diverts attention from the real cause of society's problems that affect the common people of all religions, which points to the need to unite them across the religious divide, to demand democratic and social rights, and so on.

## Appendix: Further Reflections on Communalism and Business Houses[15]

The reason for the power of saffron politics is only partly political. India's business class is not unconnected to this. The power of saffron politics also raises troubling questions about the sense of citizenship.

Commentators seem to focus on the political factors behind the success of the Modi electoral-machine. Some say that Congress has played a 'soft' Hindutva (for example, by giving tickets to some disgruntled members of Hindutva forces) or that it was not united enough. Others say that Congress' secularism has not cut much ice with the voters who fall for the communal propaganda. There is some truth in the political interpretations of the electoral success of communal politics. What is neglected in these discussions on TV and in newspapers is often what tends to be neglected in many scholarly discussions of India's polity as such: the role of business. What is the possible connection between the business houses and communal politics? Are the business houses—the so-called corporate citizens—a secular force? This issue needs to be more thoroughly investigated. I can only indicate a few things.

At the national level and in the states, the business class, by ushering in the neoliberal regime, has cleared the ground for electoral battles which are not oriented towards development, i.e. development in the sense of development for/of the poor, a process which is not primarily based on the idea that development of the poor can happen only when the business class prospers, by the so-called trickle-down mechanism. By forcing all political parties to take the free-market approach, by forcing them to pursue neoliberalism, India's business class (in solidarity with its brothers/sisters in the advanced world) have contributed to the erasure of any substantive difference between the parties. In terms of economic policies there is scarcely any difference between Congress and BJP. Even, the Left parties are not further behind in terms of following neo-liberal policies, when they have been in power. When economic policies stop being the differentiators of political parties, when all parties pursue more or less similar pro-business policies, when therefore there is a race among all parties to the top (i.e. to satisfy the needs of the business houses, giving them maximum concessions), under these conditions, parties often choose cheap identity politics to divide the electorate and win elections: Hindutva, pride based on regionalism, linguistic identity, casteism, etc.[16] By making jobs scarce, by making it difficult for ordinary toiling masses to earn a decent livelihood, neoliberalism creates the usual kind of jealousy and spirit of nasty competition among people, which take religious (and other) forms. The rise of the religious right in the last 20 years or so and the rise of corporate power under neoliberalism are not isolated from one another. Let us now come to Gujarat more specifically.

The Right has used the veneer, the appearance, of a specific style of 'development' as well as a non-secular agenda to sell its Hindutva and (sub-) nationalist politics and to benefit its business-class mentors. The veneer of development is about, among other things, bijli, sadak and pani. It is also about attracting industries and creating some jobs. It is about creating what can be called Guja-rate (the Gujarat-style rate of economic growth). Behind all this lies the fact that business houses remain attracted to Gujarat and invest there with huge subsidies from the government which increase their profit and competitive position vis-a-vis businesses located elsewhere. They have poured in millions of rupees. They like Gujarat's resources which are happily made available by its governing regime. They like Gujarat's labour, made quiet by the decisive and strong regime—it is for nothing that Mr. Modi (or Modi bhai as some business people call him) was seen as the CEO of Gujarat—a regime that boasts the lowest person-days lost in labour conflict among all the states. The good business climate of Gujarat making Guja-rate possible is created by Modi's 'determined' and 'strong' character. The business houses enjoy cordial relations with the regime. And this happens, despite the fact that the regime is the one which palpably failed to prevent the 2002 carnage of several hundred

Indian citizens who happened to be Muslims, and this was a regime which is widely seen as nurturing and protecting the elements which killed innocent people, and this was a regime much of the nationalist ideological values of which its foot soldiers valiantly shared with a masculinist fervour. The idea of so-called corporate social responsibility does not worry the business houses at all. Their business is the business of doing business. If business requires doing business with a regime that is communal and fascistic, so be it. It does not matter. To the extent that the business houses have been heavily investing in the state in their own interest which the regime boasts of[17] and to the extent that the 'development' veneer as well as communal propaganda in the electoral campaign have helped the regime came to power, the business houses—at least several of them—cannot be seen as unconnected to the political success of the regime.

It is not just this material 'support' that is important here: one must also know where the Right movement gets the money to fight elections, who funds the communal-political agenda. There is also an ideological support for the regime which comes from business houses. Ratan Tata, whose company boasts of conscious capitalism and corporate social responsibility, said: 'Modi will not have to attract people to Gujarat, it will be stupid if you are not here.' Anil Ambani was all praise for his Modi Bhai, whose various achievements he counts including the Narmada (as if all the fight against the Narmada by India's civil society was nonsense). It is this sort of business-inspired ideological support for Modi[18] and his regime—that is indeed used during the electoral campaign—that has propped up the right regime in 'popular' imagination, and this would require a detailed analysis. Those who control Gujarat's (and India's) moneybags tend to influence the mind of many voters. Ideas of those who rule economically and politically are the ideas that generally rule people's minds.

If the business forces are really for a country free from communalism, have they ever seriously considered an investment strike—at least a threat of it? A slight indication of the trouble of class politics in a state[19] makes the business class look elsewhere, but communal politics? The business class can perhaps survive with it much better than with class politics.[20] In part because communal politics helps the business class divide any possible opposition to itself from the workers' side, and because communal politics produces the sort of rightwing decisiveness that obliterates any possibility of anti-business opposition, business houses tend to enjoy comradely relations with the communal regime.

Communalism thrives on a specific irrational politics of hatred and rejection of 'the other': the idea that a person will reject his/her fellow citizens who are different from him/her in terms of religion. India's business houses—like global business houses that enjoyed doing business with South Africa's erstwhile apartheid regime or indeed Hitler's Germany until a point—do not mind doing business with a communal regime. How will the same business houses feel if the consumers start rejecting their products—a Reliance mobile or a Tata car, for example—because they are associated with a regime which spreads hate and the politics of rejection of the religious other and whose hands are stained with the blood of slaughtered citizens?

Let us move our attention from the complicity of the business class in communal politics to that of ordinary citizens. What does the electoral influence of rightwing political forces in general say about Indians as citizens of the country, and as just simple human beings? What does it say about India's democracy and the institutions of the state that are supposed to protect the secular fabric of the constitution? How can a person kill someone next to her just because she may have different religious views and engage in different religious rituals? How can one believe in the lie created by a few people that one is worse off because of his/her religion? What has happened to our education system indeed our whole ideological apparatus that is no longer able to encourage citizens of different religious identities to live in peace? What is it that makes citizens believe a political leader, when he/she treats every criticism of him/

her as a criticism of an entire province or a country or indeed an entire group following a specific religion, as if an entire province or the country belongs to him/her or to his/her party/ movement? What is it that makes one feel proud to be a citizen of a country when her fellow citizens are treated as second class citizens? What has happened to people's sense of citizenship, to solidarity? How can a person of a specific religion tolerate another person next door being cut by a mob into pieces just because she/he has a specific religion? In the context of the class of workers and peasants, the quality of one's citizenship depends on how one's fellow citizens are treated, and how one spontaneously treats other citizens. If they are treated (killed and tortured) as second class citizens by a state of whose citizen one is, then does one's citizenship not stand devalued? And what can we say about the entire set of state apparatuses, including the judiciary and the intellectual stratum, that has allowed the gradual process of capture of parts of the state and civil society by communal forces, the forces that live by spreading the idea of violence on religious grounds?

One should not be obsessed with explaining the rise of the communal forces merely by the failure of the Congress, the premier party of Indian business houses. Both are elements of a system, and both of them have to be explained, historically, by the dynamics of the political-economic system as such. The rise of the communal power is not merely an electoral rise. Therefore, to fight against them is not to be merely an electoral fight, although that is necessary to stop the communal forces making use of secular institutions of the state to further their own agenda and to communalize these institutions in a molecular fashion. The fact that the communal forces have carved out a space within the polity as such, within the state itself, and within civil society—the fact that the Right is treated as a legitimate participant in the political process and debates, including on national television—this fact, including the changes in the media, universities and judiciary, police, etc., has to be explained. In this explanation, the silent, and not so silent, role of the business houses, and changing ideological nature of the sense of citizenship in India (e.g. how do India's citizens see themselves) must be unpacked, and the business houses must be questioned on how they deal with communal regimes. They must be asked to take sides: are they on the side of communal forces or secular forces?

Also, ordinary people, i.e. the well-paid and not so well-paid members of the wage-earning and salaried strata, and small-scale producers, who constitute the majority of the nation, must ask this: are their main problems such as unemployment, employment in security, low wages, lack of housing, shelter, quality education and healthcare, etc. as well as gender and caste oppression due to the fact that in India there are Hindus and non-Hindus, or are their main problems due to the actions of the business houses, the governments of different parties, and all those communal (and casteist) forces which divide mass opposition to the business houses and the governments which fundamentally work in their interest? They must answer this question: does it matter to them whether a provincial government or indeed a national government is communal or not?

## Notes

1. The words in quotes in this paragraph are from Tagore's Gitanjali, quoted at the beginning of the book.
2. The rally in February 2016 marked the anniversary of the hanging, under suspicious conditions, of Mohammad Afzal Guru, a Kashmiri, and an accused in the terrorist attack on the parliament in 2001. The fact of the matter is that JNU students' and faculty's left leanings have been an eyesore for the right-wing ideologues and politicians. In the September 2016 student union elections, a united left front won all the four seats of the central council of the union.
3. Consider how Penguin had to withdraw the publication of Doniger's book on Hinduism due to intense pressure from the Right.
4. Interestingly, as the recent horrific incident of the rape of an 8-year-old girl, Asifa Bano, in January 2018 shows, some of the people who are defending the accused are the Hindutva forces, when in fact Hinduism will never ever support such a ghastly act.
5. Consider the logistics agreement signed in August 2016 whereby the US government can virtually use India as a military base. This is one of the most pro-imperialist actions of a government which swears by nationalism.

6. Quoted in: Marx, K. and Engels, F. (1848). *The Communist Manifesto.*
7. See a fine book, titled *Nationalism* by Thapar et al. (2016).
8. This is not at all to say that there is nothing that is scientific in the ancient Indian thinking system or scriptures. But the extent of the scientific character of the ancient ideas must be judged on the basis of contemporary scientific analysis; the fact that an idea is an ancient idea from India does not prove its scientific character (see Nanda, 2016).
9. Mr. Modi was denied for years a visa to enter the USA, the land of religious and economic freedom, for his (alleged) role in the carnage of innocent Muslims. But he was immediately embraced by Mr. Obama, the CEO of the US, on his election. The capitalist elements in the Indian diaspora in the US, who are looking for business ventures in India, played an important role in the lifting of the ban on Mr. Modi's visa.
10. In fact, specific individuals can be pro-poor, they can be sewaks of Daridra Narayan (god as manifested in the poor), as long as they are sewaks of the wider saffron structure. Many individuals in the structure can actually be very ascetic, may not have a lot of money, may in fact maintain some distance from money, and they may genuinely be interested in public service.
11. Incidentally, the saffron agenda that seeks to banish class, is also sending a grave lesson for all those who talk obsessively about cultural politics, identity politics, biopolitics, etc in abstraction from class politics or by subordinating class politics to non-class politics. In many ways, the saffron view is a continuation/extension of identity politics espoused by culturalist, post-modernist social scientists and humanities experts. The postmodern thinkers may be for democracy but the objective effect of their irrational, philosophically idealistic thinking is to produce ideological conditions, which are the breeding ground for, or which are, at least, wholly compatible with, the saffron thinking, and which are anti-democratic.
12. These include: growing unemployment, and rising inequality, that capitalism creates but cannot solve, and that too in an economically backward imperialized peripheral-capitalist country.
13. These include the idea that plastic surgery happened in India thousands of years ago (and this means that India is so great that whatever modern science has achieved, much of which has been achieved in India already). These also include the idea that, and as mentioned before, such and such god or goddess or their assistant was born in, and/or visited, place x or place y, and that these places must be defended against non-Hindus, even by violently destroying any structure which may lie there which is of the non-Hindu type. The ideas about plastic surgery, birthplaces of gods, and their extraordinary powers, and so on are actually great ideas. These are great ideas for fictional writings: they actually show the imagination of the writer which is a reflection of the ambition of people living in a rich culture that existed a long

time ago, the ambition to, for example, transcend the bounds of time and place, and of the human body. These ideas should be a source of great literary enjoyment. But must they be treated as real (unless these ideas have been proven by science to be real), and be the basis for mobilizing people for votes and for power? One can actually see that while one aim of this sort of saffron thinking is to suggest that India's culture (or more specifically, Hindu culture), has been rich, the actual effect of such thinking might be the opposite: someone who says that Indians practised modern plastic surgery many centuries ago would not be trusted when she/he says that Indians invented yoga and ideas in mathematics, etc. that have much scientific value indeed. It is absolutely acceptable to feel proud of a society's past and its achievements, including those who spent thousands of hours meditating, interacting with nature and serving people, in order to discipline their minds, to learn about nature and social arrangements, and who shared some ideas about the human mind, human society and nature. Some of them can be actually scientifically verifiable and put to good use, and people of the world would be grateful that those ideas came from a region called India, just as people admire the fact that many useful ideas came from ancient Greece. That does not mean that everything people have said thousands of years ago must be true, and that does not mean that someone who criticizes them is an anti-national or anti-Hindu. In fact, if these people learnt anything, it was on the basis of discussion, debate and criticisms, as Professor Sen (2005) has shown.

14. Of course, the capitalist system is also supported and managed by non-saffron political parties.
15. This is a revised version of Das (2010).
16. In fact, fighting anti-incumbency requires the use of identity politics.
17. Whether this 'development' helps the rural and urban poor in any significant economically and ecologically sustainable manner is another matter.
18. It is not necessarily useful to single out a person such as Mr. Modi for India's communal situation, although when individuals are responsible that should be highlighted. A given person is the manifestation of a broader process which is what the Right movement is about, and which is, in turn, ultimately connected to the nature of the bourgeois class. That class (along with its hangers-on in the middle class) is fine with communal carnage—just as it is fine with massive poverty and child malnutrition, etc,—as long as it can make money and loads of money. A fuller analysis of the communal situation will include an analysis of such things as: Indian capitalism with its own specificities as a part of (crisis-ridden) global capitalism, supported by imperialist powers seeking to convert some countries in the periphery into its junior partners; the political power and political ideas that support such a

communal-bourgeois system; specific groups/organizations and mass movements (including those that are explicitly political and those that claim to be cultural and welfare-oriented but perform deeply political functions propping up a Right regime), and finally, specific individuals endowed with resources and bourgeois-communal ideas who want to make a difference to the communal-bourgeois cause. To be added, of course, to this 'list' is the failure of democratic and socialist/left movements to fight for democratic demands and economic concessions as a part of a broader fight for a society where resources are collectively controlled for the collective purpose.

19. Consider de-industrialization of Bengal in the light of its culture trade union strikes, especially, before the 1990s.
20. This is even if there is a real danger of communal politics leading to widespread destruction of property and to public order issues.

# 8

# People's Poverty vs 'Poverty of Left Theory/Practice'

It is widely known that India has a massive problem of poverty. Millions of people do not have the resources to satisfy their need for food and to meet their other basic needs, such as decent shelter, quality education and healthcare. Yet, in terms of aggregate (not per capita) private wealth, India is one of the richest countries. This means that the country does have the resources to satisfy people's needs but it fails to do so. In other words: there is a visible contradiction between the objectively-existing ability of the system to satisfy people's basic needs and the fact that people's needs remain unmet.

## Class Analysis and Poverty

The problem of poverty can be explained in many ways. The fact that in some cases individuals do not behave or take responsibility for their lives is cited as a reason.[1] Sometimes, the low level of literacy is shown as a factor. It is also widely believed that the market system produces problems such as temporary unemployment or under-investment in social sectors, the problems that governments can address, but because of corruption in the government or because of inadequate government intervention, the problems remain. Some point to caste oppression. Others blame crony capitalism—the fact that some companies take undue advantage of their connection with powerful politicians and/or government officials and therefore raise the cost of what they sell above the average cost, or do not obey the laws which should otherwise help workers a bit. Sometimes environmental factors are also seen as a contributory factor.

These explanations are partial and inadequate. A fuller explanation must stress the class character of society: the issues surrounding who controls society's resources and whether resources are used for private profit or to satisfy human need. When someone goes to work, what they get paid is much less than their net contribution to the final product, and ultimately profit comes from this difference between what workers produce and what they get in wages. In fact, from such a gap only does profit of business people come at the level of society as a whole. When wages fall below a level, ordinary people fail to meet their needs. In backward capitalist countries such as India, the economic system is more or less based on a regime of long hours and low wages: given that there are millions of unemployed and underemployed people, employers are under no economic compulsion to raises wages. If one refuses to work for less, another can be hired easily. Besides, in order to cut costs, in certain sectors, labour-displacing technology is used, and this causes unemployment or under-employment, which in turn can produce low income.

And in fact India remains competitive in the global economy on the basis of an economic regime of low wages and long hours. When people lose access to their land and other resources which are grabbed by the big business, then people are vulnerable to poverty. We have also seen that small-scale producers are vulnerable to being economically unviable, and that can cause low income and therefore poverty.

In short, India's contemporary political economy, which underlies its massive poverty, is based on the following:

a) a regime of low wages and long hours, made possible due to a massive army of under- and unemployed people, which contributes to India being a low-wage platform for global capitalism;

b) a regime of transfer of resources at an extremely cheap rate from small-scale producers, from the commons (common land, water and forests, etc.), and from the state-owned sector, which used to provide some employment, to the privately-owned profit-seeking domestic and foreign big businesses;

c) an unsustainable use of natural resources that contributes to the low-cost production of commodities for sale for profit (this means profit comes at the expense of the environment as society is not fully compensated for by the business houses for using the natural resources);

d) growing inability of the state to assist the poor as more and more of its resources are being used to subsidize business people and as it is starving itself of resources by not taxing the business houses;

e) impact of imperialism on Indian economy and society (including actions of MNCs and of governments of rich and powerful countries);

f) all the above being sustained in the face of massive resistance from common people, through coercion and through strategies of granting meagre and reversible material concessions, and of dividing the masses on the basis of gender, caste, religion, location, etc.

India's political economy underlying its massive poverty is full of contradictions: the contradiction between business owners and workers; between business owners and small-scale producers; between the business owners and the environment; between the state of the propertied classes and the poor who are from the working class and small scale producer class background, and so on.

## Left Practice

In the backdrop of these numerous important contradictions, there is another set of contradictions we must consider, the contradictions surrounding the Left itself: the contradiction between its rhetoric/theory and its practice, and the contradiction between its existing theory/practice and the kind of theory/practice required to eradicate poverty and solve other burning problems. To the extent that ideas can produce a material effect by reacting back on the material world, the contradiction-ridden objective material conditions for poverty just briefly discussed above—this material world of poverty—are reproduced partly through problematic ideas subscribed to by the Left and their attendant political practice. In particular, the poverty of Left theory and practice and theory of poverty must be considered together in their mutual interconnection.

Let us consider the extent to which the Naxalite movement as an important component of the Left—as a political practice—has an effect on poverty. It is an ideological success of the broader movement, including the mainstream Left movement, that the Naxalite movement is not seen any more merely as a law and order issue even by some members of the political establishment. It is rather seen as one that is rooted in the worsening crisis of the system and in mass poverty. But does the practice of the Naxalite movement, in turn, affect poverty? This is a difficult question to answer. One can only say that the Naxalite movement is a contingent product of a series of contradictions underlying poverty as mentioned above (see Das, 2009) and that this movement itself has had a contradictory effect on the 'landscape of poverty'. In some places, the Naxalite movement—like other types of Left movement—has played a developmental role, however limited it may be (e.g. taking land from big landlords and distributing it among poor people; encouraging small-scale irrigation; making state officials do their duty, etc.) (Das, 2017b). The movement has established educational facilities, built small-scale irrigational facilities, etc. In fact, in addition to the use of arms by some sections of the Naxalite movement, it is this success that angers the state so much. This is because it is the developmental success of the Naxalites and other similar formations that leads to their popularity among the masses and to many of their organic intellectuals (ibid.). Concomitantly, this situation may have created a legitimacy crisis of the state in specific localities: the perception that the state has failed to do what non-state radical

actors are able to. The limited military power of sections of the movement is enhanced by their developmental success. That the state is really worried about the ideological support[2] for the Naxalites is indicated by its increasingly repressive attitude, even with respect to intellectuals and activists who have nothing to do with Maoism (more on this below). It is also not difficult to see that the Left movement in general and the Naxalite movement in particular have prompted various development policies of the state (from which the poor have received some succour, if not a lot): developmental policies are generally undertaken in response to potential and/or actual struggle, and this struggle has been conducted by the Naxalite left (and other sections of the Left).

In other places, the conflict between sections of the Naxalite movement and the government has resulted in the destruction of the limited developmental infrastructure that existed. This is bound to have a negative effect on poverty alleviation, other factors being constant. Given the corrupt nature of the state which is a major barrier to the implementation of government policies on the ground which the masses have fought for, and given the increasingly pro-business character of the state, which has been withdrawing from the limited amount of welfare activities it was engaged in earlier, when a school building is destroyed by Maoist forces, it almost vanishes forever. It is unlikely to be rebuilt anytime soon by the corrupt neoliberal state practising austerity. The rural landscape has been thus politicized. An empty school building offers an opportunity for security forces fighting 'left extremists' to use it as a base. And, because of the way in which it is used by security forces, the 'left extremists' sometimes destroy it. Indeed, state actors are also involved in a similar destruction while trying to clear a place of these extremists and force ordinary people to leave the place and live elsewhere (e.g. camps); of course, arguably one aim of this 'political gentrification' (clearance) is to make room for businesses to do their business (e.g. mining, etc.).

There is another kind of dynamics here. In a few places, democratic organization of exploited classes has had some mitigating effect on poverty (e.g. in the form of lower wages, increased government benefits). There is evidence that the new employment guarantee scheme, which the Congress government put in place (rather reluctantly), partly thanks to the effort of the mainstream Left and other progressive groups and individuals (including from civil society), works somewhat better where the poor people are able to monitor the workings of the programme in an organized manner. But the state tends to increasingly Naxalize all forms of radical class-based democratic organization. A radical movement is given a Naxalite (or increasingly, Maoist) label by the state. This 'social-constructivist' act justifies the repression and destruction of the people involved in the movement by the state as well as by 'non- or semi-state' actors supported by it (e.g. 'civil society' militia). This is a post-modern performative political act by the post-colonial state: 'I think you are a Maoist, so you are a Maoist'. Therefore, the Naxalite movement may have what can be called an unintended negative consequence on poverty-alleviation as well as on fights against gender and caste inequalities and ecological degradation. But at the same time, state repression will contribute to the Naxalite cause. So, 'if I think you are a Maoist (when you are not), you are likely to become a Maoist'.[3]

The actual balance between these two tendencies—poverty being reinforced and poverty being mitigated by the Naxalite movement—is, partly, a matter of the place-specific balance of power between the forces of the state, representing the capitalist-landlord-imperialist system, and the exploited masses, some of whom are indeed led by the Naxalites.[4] This geography of power and poverty is an interesting issue, whose concrete nature needs empirical investigation. Yet, what cannot be denied is that Naxalites of various types are, in part through their political practice, raising important issues—'internal colonization' of tribals, oppression of women and lower castes, police repression, bureaucratic corruption, dispossession of peasants, landlessness, exploitation by landlords and traders, etc. They, along with other sections of the radical movement, are stepping into the space more or less vacated by the mainstream

Left. That their ideology and their method of struggle are problematic is a separate matter.

I now turn to the practice of the mainstream Left, one which is, more or less, primarily election-oriented. The mainstream Left, at least in its early history (1960s, and 1970s) has, by using both extra-parliamentary mobilization and employing state institutions, partially fought against the remnants of feudalism and distributed land to millions of needy people (Das, 1997; Kohli, 1987; Herring, 1983). It has played an important role in forcing the central government to introduce progressive legislations (NREGS; Forest Act, etc.), and without its involvement, perhaps more sectors of the economy will be in private hands than is the case now, which would have had more adverse consequences on the poor. Yet, in terms of extra-parliamentary mobilization, its role has been muted in more recent times. Here I mainly refer to the Left leadership, and not necessarily to those who are common members of Left parties and who actively fight on the ground against exploitation and oppression.

It seems that the Left has limited time to politically act, outside the halls of the law-making process, on all those issues that matter to ordinary people. Most of their political energy is directed at winning seats, as opposed to politically winning the hearts and minds of the masses, through mass movements and through what Lenin called political exposure, in his *What is To Be Done*. But elections do not happen every day. Further, big business has to be courted for development to happen in the places where the Left is or has been in power. Such development is necessary for political legitimacy, and it is also apparently necessary to create a working class which would be mobilized against the capitalist class some time in the distant future.[5] And, if the Left government, where the Left was/is in control over the provincial branches of the nation-state, does not court big business, non-Left governments will. This partly explains why there is rather a limited amount of difference in practice between the Left ruling in a province and non-Left parties: the capitalist logic has levelled the crucial political differences between the ruling Left and ruling non-Left formations. And the capitalist-political system sets limit to the extent to which social democracy even of the most Leftist variety can be practised within a bounded territory in a country. The Left is always in danger of being 'left out' (of genuine Left practice) when it becomes a part of the state which it cannot but administer fundamentally in the interest of the property owners. Social democracy in one province is increasingly difficult, given the ability and the inclination of capital to move across provinces.

## Left Theory

The hallmark of Marxist theory is this (see Das, 2014a: Chapter 2; Das, 2017a: Chapters 5-6): that class relations, and in contemporary times, capitalist class relations (which are associated with the development of productive forces), are the most fundamental cause of major social problems (e.g. poverty; undemocratic practices), that capitalist class relations subordinate, and make use of, other contributory causes (e.g. caste; gender, etc.) of major problems to its own logic, that the capitalist state's fundamental duty is to oppress/suppress the masses and keep them from challenging property relations in any basic way, that there are severe limits to the extent to which the state and capitalists can grant concessions to the masses and that both indeed are increasingly turning authoritarian in the face of a potential and actual social struggles (especially as capitalism as a global system is in decline). And Marxist theory says that capitalism along with the remnants of any pre/non-capitalist relations that may exist must be abolished (as opposed to reformed/regulated) through the struggle of proletarians in an alliance with poor peasants and other sections of the low-income small-scale property-owning groups, to create conditions where a sustained and permanent solution to major problems can begin at multiple scales, as a part of the process of the (global) onslaught against capitalism.

Contrast this broad theoretical vision to the reality of Left theoretical practice. At the risk of a certain amount of exaggerating and without intending to under-value the intellectual contributions of the Left relative to what is achieved, say, within the movement of the Right (or indeed the Centre), let me say this: the absence of serious and consistent engagement with historical materialism as a theory and its political vision—and particularly ideas of Marx rooted in such works as *Capital*[6]—is increasingly what characterizes most of what can be described as Left culture (this includes election-oriented Left and other formations). Where in India can one find a serious semester-long postgraduate level course on *Das Kapital* offered by a Leftist scholar? In some Left circles, the Kaleckis and the Keyenes are in fact studied and referred to, more than the Karl Marxes. Much, if not all, of what goes on in the name of Marxism is at best a kind of radical nationalism, or radical sub-nationalism (provincialism), with a touch of a democratic vision (tasks that connect to the interests of broader sections of the people and different classes including property-owners). More specifically, much of what is Marxist theory in India is a healthy soup of: anti-feudalism, anti-imperialism, anti-communalism, and with a slight touch of social-democratic reformism.[7] There is not much systematic theoretical discussion on materialism and dialectics, on class relations, class consciousness, political economy, nature of peripheral capitalism, etc.

Rigorous regular discussions on Marxist theory, including ideas from Marx, Lenin, Trotsky, Luxemburg, etc. among many scholars are rare (as compared to what is observed in Western Marxism, for example). While there is some direct engagement with Marx and Lenin (and that too, in a very selected and perfunctory manner),[8] and Mao[9], there is effectively little discussion on Trotsky (or Luxemburg). Isn't there anything in the voluminous work of these writers that one can appreciate?

In terms of political economy, much of India's Marxist intellectual work is more or less an empirical critique of the excesses of capitalism, and often from the standpoint of the weaker sections of the property-owning strata, or the standpoint of class relations that are not capitalist. Let us return to the question of poverty. Within the Left discourse as elsewhere, there is plenty of useful discussion on matters which are of a more concrete nature: for example, how many people are poor (read: destitutes); the various strata within the category of 'the poor'; how the number of the poor rises and falls (in relation to some contingent and proximate factors); and in terms of 'causality', what is the degree of association between poverty and, for example, land-holding or caste status, etc.[10] The stress, more or less, is on the surface appearances of the landscape of poverty. But if the appearance were the reality, there would be no need for science, Marx commented in *Capital* Vol. 3. If there is so much persistent poverty, it is dominantly seen by much of the Left as existing because of wrong policies, and wrong manner of policy implementation (e.g. corruption, too much concentration of power at the federal level, and so on). Sometimes, it is seen as due to the excesses of the capitalist social formation, including so-called feudal remnants, and unequal distribution of land and other resources, and small-scale producers losing their land. The stress, in more recent times, is also on how neoliberalism is affecting the poor, how withdrawal of government support for the poor is affecting them. What this approach—which is not strictly speaking wrong, but which is limited—means in most cases is that a better-regulated capitalism is possible and that it will address poverty and other issues. Poverty is seen as persisting because of the wrong way in which the state managers (and their intellectual friends in the universities which are increasingly enthralled by neoliberalism) conceptualize and act on the problem. In the existing popular, propaganda and intellectual discourses of the Left on poverty, etc., it often appears as if the state and its conjunctural policies hang in mid air, without a firm root in the soil of capitalist class relations, national and international. Very rarely do we hear arguments about how the capitalist mode of production and exchange are internally connected to poverty and other social problems. Very rarely is poverty seen as a consequence of class, of capitalist class relations, of the multiple contradictions of the capitalist totality, which I referred to, the totality of exchange, property and value relations. What escapes the target of theoretical critique from the Left therefore is the capitalist class as such (and especially, the domestic capitalist class), and its state, in terms of their fundamental conditions of existence and class-character, as opposed to their mere excesses. What is therefore missing is a critique of the type that does not allow for the reproduction of the system in a slightly modified form and that demands—or at least, makes the ideological-political preparation for demanding and not indefinitely postponing—the transcendence of the system, a critique that is intransigent.[11]

While political actions of the Naxalite Left appear to be, and in some places, are militant, their theory of Indian society is also severely deficient. The idea subscribed to by many Naxalite groups that India is a semi-feudal country and not yet a dominantly capitalist country is absolutely inadequate. This is because they conflate capitalism-as-a-class relation with an imagined (high) level of development of productive forces traditionally seen in the West and/or with the universal use of free-wage labour. If the theory of India not being a capitalist country is correct, then it follows that the capitalist class, whose prime interests the state represents, does not play an important role in creating poverty. Both the premise and the conclusion are wrong. And, if the social system is not dominantly capitalist, it follows that the proletarian does not really exist as the main anti-capitalist agent and that urban spaces, the spaces of capital, are not the real stage for the drama of radical social change. The idea that India is not yet a dominantly capitalist social formation implies that mobilization of the masses against the root of the problems (i.e. the capitalist class relation) and for a workers' and peasants' government is not possible, and all one can do is not to fight against capitalism itself, but to fight for a better form of capitalism (one that is more democratic and more developed).

The main theoretical problem of the Left may be stated as thus: there is a need for theorizing much more rigorously and much more consistently the internal connection between India's capitalist class relations and its social problems, within a multi-scalar framework, than is the case now. Often it is the case that:

what is most difficult to achieve is most necessary to achieve. We must ask whether there are regular and geographically widespread theoretical discussions on such topics as: class relations, nature of (peripheral) capitalism, nature of capitalism in new and old forms of agrarian production; the nature of the relation between capitalist class relations and gender/caste relations and relations of indigeneity, etc. Perhaps there is a need for another round of debate on the mode of production, and this time, not on the mode of production in agriculture but in India as a whole and in its different regions. We must also ask whether there are regular theoretical discussions on: the nature of revolutionary agency, the peripheral-capitalist state, new imperialism, capitalism-inflicted metabolic rift causing massive environmental damage to land, water and forest resources, capitalist ideology including commodity and capital fetishism, the capitalist character of religious fundamentalism and casteism, etc.? A rigorous theoretical understanding of these issues, informed by a radical philosophy of dialectics which helps one unpack the totalizing logic of capitalism and its ways of operation in India, will allow concrete analyses of poverty (of different groups and in different places).

The reality is multilayered. Given this, would it not be interesting to ask: a) what are the general mechanisms by which capitalism works, b) what are the forms of those mechanisms in India—what mechanisms sustain/reproduce and undermine capitalism in India, c) what are the effects of these mechanisms on poverty (and other problems/processes), and d) how these effects are experienced differentially in different places and by different social-cultural groups experiencing various forms of oppression, and d) what transformational possibilities does the present-day contradiction-ridden, poverty-causing capitalism in India poses for the Left?

Turning to capital's 'other', the proletarian and semi-proletarian masses of India are not just a suffering mass. They are also a fighting-mass. Whether it is in the auto industry in North India or factories in export-oriented places in South India or rural areas of Odisha where capital has sought to dispossess people, the masses have always shown their ability to fight capitalism and social oppression. How is the internal composition of the class changing, and what is holding back its emergence as a class at the national scale,[12] as a part of the international working class? To ask questions about the poverty-causing mechanisms of capitalism is also to ask questions about the poverty-fighting agent in the system (i.e. the proletariat), which condenses in itself the sufferings of all other sections of the working mass including poor peasants. The Left must ask fundamental questions about the nature of the obstacles to the transformation of trade unionist type consciousness into class-consciousness and about the nature of the obstacles to the working class resistance to capitalism in India. It should be stressed that there is a massive contradiction between the objective conditions (poverty and economic backwardness, crisis and its continuing effects, etc.) that are conducive to the possibility of a massive ideological and political opposition to the system on the one hand, and the subjective preparations of the masses to launch such an opposition on the other. Such a contradiction is partly because of the fact that there are objective conditions created by capitalism itself (e.g. exploitation in the workplace, immiserization, competition in the labour market where jobs are increasingly scarce, lack of access to a minimum level of education, geographically uneven development with unequal conditions of existence across regions, etc.) that weaken and divide the masses. Capitalism that needs to be opposed does create obstacles to the opposition. Then there are the ideological and coercive actions of the state. There are also various political parties of the propertied class at the national and provincial scales, that divide the masses electorally, etc., and India has many of these parties. The actual experience of the masses in relation to gender, caste, indigeneity, ethnicity, etc. is dividing them, sometimes without much direct assistance from the ruling elites, as the masses make use of these relations in their self-interest as they see it.[13] Then, of course, there are the ideologies and actions of trade union bureaucrats/leaders and reformism in left parties that obfuscate class consciousness and restricts it to narrow bounds (e.g. trade unionist consciousness).

It is only the development of a rigorous Marxist theory with due attention to concrete conditions in India and South Asia as parts of the world-economy and world-polity, that can help the Left make sense of not only the nature of capitalism that needs to be fought but also the conditions under which the masses will be prepared to fight. There is an urgent need to raise the issues of class exploitation and oppression in the theoretically correct way, and at the appropriate geographical scale. Even in the 21st century India, as mentioned earlier, it is interesting that several Left thinkers have doubts that India is a dominantly capitalist country. It is necessary to reflect on the extent to which the origin of rural suffering lies in rural areas and on the extent to which the conditions of peasants can be merely understood in terms of their relations with rural property owners in abstraction from the overall capitalist system including capitalist class-relations and the capitalist state.

Consider the theory concerning the democratic and the 'new' national questions. To a certain extent poverty is caused by the fact that there are undemocratic practices and by the fact that Indian society is being subjugated to imperialist economic forces such as the policies of the World Bank (which is an aspect of the new national question in the 'post-colonial' times). Marx and Lenin's works and contemporary political economy teach us that: capital rules through a variable combination of both repressive measures and democratic consent-generating methods. It rules through various forms of social oppression. Although neutral at an abstract level, in the concrete sense, capital is not—and can never be—neutral towards social difference (e.g. gender and caste/ethnic/regional, etc. oppression): by treating sections of workers and poor peasants as second-class citizens, as less than human, can capital achieve these goals: a) lower the cost of production, and b) discipline and punish the people it hires.[14] One does not eat caste or gender. They exist for a material-political reason. All kinds of feudal remnants and extra-economic coercion exist that moneybags make use of to make more money. These undemocratic processes have real implications for capital's political-economic projects. Why do we not get it? Capital understands it well. Capital can tolerate a certain level of democracy, including a peaceful change of government, through elections, as long as the change is from one bourgeois regime to another. So capital is never neutral with respect to the form of democracy: for example, capital will not tolerate the demand that workers' committees audit companies in which they work, or that electoral constituencies be created on the basis of class. It is interesting that certain constituencies in India are reserved for only Scheduled Castes or Scheduled Tribes: electoral candidates can only belong to these social groups. Can constituencies be reserved as well for candidates from working class and poor peasants' backgrounds, who will raise issues that specifically affect these classes and offer solutions from their own class-standpoint? Capital will never allow this. Capital can also never be neutral with respect to the undemocratic practices of state actors: capital makes use of, and, contributes to, the undemocratic functioning of its state. Think about all the secret deals it strikes with politicians and officials when it acquires peasants' land or how it disobeys the state's rules about workplace safety. A state that is open to day-to-day democratic influence from the masses will not be a capitalist state structure. Its officials/politicians cannot be as corrupt as they are without the capitalist context. Neither is capital even neutral with respect to landlord exploitation: landlords tend to be allies of capital because of their ability to control the rural masses, which is partly why urban capital tends to make compromises with rural landlords: capital is fearful that any fight against landlords can spill over to become a fight against itself. Many landed elites actually invest in capitalist ventures (e.g. transportation), and many urban business people invest in rural landownership. Similarly, given that the so-called national capital has become a junior partner of imperialists,[15] will any successful fight against imperialism be allowed by national capital? Can, therefore, any successful fight against imperialism not also require a fight against national capital?[16] Capital is a social relationship. It is a social power. It is not about a given magnitude or locational origin of the means of production: in what sense is 'national' capital—or any given section of it—necessarily any less exploitative than imperialist capital?

These theoretical issues also raise political questions, and we are now dialectically back to Left practice, briefly. If capitalism makes use of, and benefits from, undemocratic practices,[17] to what extent is it possible to successfully fight for more political democracy and against social oppression, landlordism and indeed against imperialism (represented by the World Bank, etc.) in the contemporary situation without also fighting against capitalism as a relation, as a social power? How does one assess the various kinds of micro-politics[18] vis-a-vis total politics based on the shoulder of the working class and semi-proletarians who together are the largest single class and who produce the wealth that is converted into profit and interest, etc.? They possess a massive amount of class-political power. If they stop working, the production of profit stops. If we take the class power of the working class seriously, how do we assess the violent tactic resorted to by some sections of the Naxalite movement, and especially, if the tasks at hand are seen by the movement as more democratic and less anti-capitalistic? What should one make of Lenin's point that: 'without the working people, all bombs are powerless, patently powerless'? Is individual-level terrorism not useless?

Indeed, to what extent is it the case that micro-political fights (fights against this or that issue, this or that part of the propertied-class, and not confronting capital as such) and fights that are merely on the local and provincial basis have created all kinds of illusions among the radicals and left-liberals, the illusions about the possibility of reforms on behalf of the poor? How many times do the Left governments talk about federal constraints on what they can do? If there are severe constraints, how do we assess the importance of the Left being a part of the bourgeois state?

There is a need for a real democratic, friendly, polite and non-antagonistic discussion of radical ideas among all kinds of Left formations and intellectuals, ideas about class and class politics broadly understood (i.e. a class politics that is also sensitive to questions of caste, gender, nationality, and environment), which will inform radical action. The aim of such discussions would be to create conditions for the production of a non-sectarian revolutionary theory that is compatible with and that feeds into a 'united front', democratically-organized, struggle by the masses—a struggle against the profit-driven system that exploits and oppresses the majority and where democracy more or less means the democracy for those who have money and muscle power—a united front of multiple Left parties existing separately and striking together.

To ask the sorts of theoretical questions I have alluded to and indeed many other similar questions and to address them, theoretically and with a practical intent, there must be a process of development of, and interest, in theoretical issues (with an eye towards the concrete situation and practical action) on the part of a large critical mass of people, including university students and teachers, educated elements working in factories and offices, educated people from the villages, etc. Here is the enormous potential of Left reading groups (e.g. the groups that will read and discuss, with a critical intent, not only *Capital* but also *What is To Be Done, April Theses, Imperialism, Revolution Betrayed, Permanent Revolution, Reform or Revolution,* and other works of permanent value). Without the reading groups and similar fora, which can exist as a part of the process of active political mobilization, it can be said that India's Left cultural atmosphere will remain poverty-stricken.[19]

The state of affairs under discussion—i.e. absence of an adequate theoretical critique of capitalism and its connection to mass poverty—arguably and partly reflects a singular failure of the Left (the Left movement and the Left-in-power): to raise the level of radical-theoretical advancement of the cadre, sympathizers and progressive-radical university students.[20] That is not all. I agree that the issue of 'poverty of theory' within the Left is a difficult issue to tackle, especially in a country with mass poverty and associated low level of education and culture.[21] The entire blame for the state of affairs under discussion (i.e. lack of theoretical –critical engagement) cannot be on the Left itself or indeed on its leadership. That would be too subjective a judgement and too harsh. We have to eat before we can think. That the majority of the people of India, which is incidentally one of the richest nations in terms of aggregate private wealth,[22] are not able to eat adequately and that people's most basic needs remain less-than-satisfied and that outside big cities, to find a recent book on an aspect of theory of capitalism or some such topic is difficult, all these perhaps contribute to a kind of anti-intellectualism (and anti-theory), that is often inimical to theoretical discussion in general. For many: theoretical becomes = academic = abstract = impractical. Those who believe in this, however, forget that they are also coming from a given theoretical perspective, the hallmark of which is empiricism, a theoretical attitude that panders to the fetishization of what is on the surface.

## Conclusion

The problem of poverty is pregnant with political possibilities. The poor people do not control the means of production or do not control in a sufficient quantity and are therefore subjected to exploitation. Their poverty must be seen as a form of systemic violence: the class system snatches the means of subsistence and means of production from them. The system deprives the masses of the fruits of their own labour. Poverty must be seen as dominantly a product of various types of class contradictions in the class system, including contradictions surrounding the capitalist state, whose poverty-alleviating intervention is severely limited by its class character. Yet, the poor are not just sufferers. They also fight against their conditions, the class contradictions. The Left movement—in theory and practice—has helped the poor in their fight. However, is what it does in theory and practice adequate to fight material inadequacies called poverty? It is important to ask questions about the extent to which poverty of the masses is partly linked to the poverty (i.e. inadequacy) of theory/practice of the Left in India. In particular, if poverty is fundamentally caused by capitalist class contradictions, does the Left in India take capitalist class relations seriously enough, intellectually and politically?

The answer is that a lot needs to be done. Here there is a contradiction at work. The Left exists, in India as in nearly every other country, to fight against the material (as well as political and cultural) conditions producing various forms of injustice such as massive, unavoidable and multidimensional poverty. Yet, these conditions themselves create barriers to the development of Left theory and Left thinking. Development of theory, and its dissemination in simple language, are necessary for the Left to mobilize its forces and fight the system in the most democratic way the system allows it to. Whether this can happen will decide if the common people will continue to experience near-barbaric level of deprivation and an attack on their democratic rights or if they will experience a life that is under their collective control and that is qualitatively better, more humane, more democratic, more satisfying, more dignified. Given the massive size of the proletarian and semi-proletarian forces and self-employed small-scale producers in India (close to at least 1000 million), an onslaught by them on capitalism and its state and on the forces using caste and religion to divide the masses and to inflict violence on low castes and religious minorities, would be a beacon to radical forces in other countries, both rich and poor. Therefore, the Indian anti-capitalist, proletarian Left has a global political responsibility. Only time will tell if it can discharge such a responsibility.[23]

## Notes

1. Sometimes, a communal colour is added when it is said that in certain communities women have more children, and that contributes to poverty.
2. This is not to be confused with theoretical support, support for their theory.

3. The imperialist policy of pre-emptive strikes against weaker Third World governments which may challenge imperialists slightly bit is employed by the capitalist class and its state in a Third World country such as India against any group within the nation that challenges capitalist hegemony. What is at stake here is the state's monopoly not over physical coercion within a given territory but over the very definition of what is good for the nation (and who counts as a part of the nation). When that monopoly is resisted, the state fights back ruthlessly.
4. It is another matter that how the masses are exactly led—militarily or politically—is a different matter.
5. Indeed, what I will call 'distant-ism'—the idea that the real struggle against capitalism will happen in the distant future—unites nearly all the sections of the Left. Such a strategy breaks the link between the fight for concessions and the fight for transcending the existing profit-driven system.
6. The recent publication of a short title, Marx's *Capital: An Introductory Reader* edited by Prabhat Patnaik (2011) is a welcome initiative.
7. This is the central tendency of the Left thinking, and not the outliers of whom there are many brilliant examples.
8. Note how the rigorous discussion on Capital is missing in much Marxist political economy except for Lenin's *One Step Forward, Two Steps Back*. Scant attention is paid to his *April Theses* where he made a definite connection between the struggle for democracy and the struggle for a new society, a society that is not profit-driven.
9. Although there seems to be a particular stress put on his military type writings rather than on his political-economic and philosophical writings.
10. Undoubtedly all these are important issues. But they must be seen in relation to the capitalist totality.
11. Of course, sometimes criticisms against imperialist capitalist forces are heard. There are scholars such as Prabhat Patnaik who have regularly written about the adverse effects of (new) imperialism on India. Even then some elements of the Left apparently look forward to—or at least would not mind—closer economic connections with the supreme imperialist power of the world (as per a recent wiki cable discussed in *The Hindu*).
12. Marx indicates in *Poverty of Philosophy* that a class becomes a political force in its struggle with capital really at the national scale, as opposed to local scale.
13. This is not to say that: the ruling class elements and their political and ideological spokespersons do not fan the fire of these divisions or that capitalism does not structurally promote divisive identities based on non-class relations.

14. This is, of course, not to entirely reduce caste and gender to capitalist exploitation.
15. This is so pronounced that when world masters talk about giving a role to India in international affairs, Indian capitalists and the middle class become euphoric.
16. National capital here does not include people working in their own factories or offices (or farms) (and they may even hire a couple of people, sometimes for only a part of the year) in order to be able to generate a revenue so they can pay their bills for a living.
17. These include unequal gender and caste relations, unequal landholdings, extra-economic coercion, and these arguably include as well massive absolute poverty that makes it impossible to exercise democratic rights in any genuine manner. Absolute poverty must be seen as a democratic question.
18. This includes class-fractional politics—i.e. the fight against this section of the property-owning class and not that.
19. This is offered as an internal critique in part because everyone—including myself—who thinks she/he is on the Left directly or indirectly reproduces this poverty of Left theory.
20. Of course, this fault cannot be laid at the door of the sections of the Left for whom radical theoretical consciousness among ordinary people, the masses, is not of much relevance, because they do not believe in self-emancipation of the poor.
21. And here by poverty of theory I am referring to poverty in its relative sense: there is an enormous gap between the amount of theoretical critique of the system that is necessary and what happens actually; I am not at all saying that there is no radical theoretical, class-based, analysis of poverty, etc.
22. According to New World Wealth (reported in *Times of India* on May 31, 2016), India is ranked seventh, ahead of Canada ($4,700 billion), Australia ($4,500 billion) and Italy ($4,400 billion), in terms of net private wealth. India's total individual wealth is $5,200 billion.
23. While any major success of the Indian Left may be a beacon to the Left elsewhere, it is also true that the Indian Left can only achieve genuine success on the basis of close collabouration with the Left in other countries, given capitalism's global nature and given the fact that national economies are increasingly interconnected.

# 9

# The Class Character of the Indian State, and the Poor

## A Long-Term View*

As widely known, India has been experiencing a relatively high economic growth rate since the 1990s. Many believe that India is an emerging economic superpower. But India's traditional image of a country afflicted by mass poverty remains. There is a material basis for such an image. The majority lack access to nutritious food as well as housing, education, and health care, and this is the case in spite of some achievements, such as an increase in life expectancy, literacy levels and income, in the general population. India still lives in villages, and its villagers—rural wage-earners and small-scale, self-employed producers—are poor. Given all this, one is compelled to ask: is India an economic power house or a poor house? And if it is a poor house, the question is: why?

To answer this question, one can look at the way the private sector economy works. I will, however, focus attention on the Indian state,[1] and argue that an important reason for the continuing problem of poverty is that the state has, more

---

* This Chapter contains ideas from my work on state theory, class theory, and the Indian state (Das, 2006; 2007; 2009; 2017a). The content of the Chapter was shared in two lectures: the first C.P. Singh Memorial lecture that I delivered at the National Association of Geographers of India Conference, December 2-4, 2005 in Bangalore, and a lecture I delivered at the Development Research Institute on January 7, 2017 at Utkal University, Bhubaneswar, Odisha. I am grateful to many scholars who provided critical feedback.

or less, failed to implement its own anti-poverty policies. I will briefly discuss four major anti-poverty interventions in rural areas, and I will then show that there are some general processes underlying their failure.

## Thinking About the State in India

The Indian state has been seen in various ways. In the 1980s, the Rudolphs from Chicago looked at the Indian state as a third actor which has supposedly marginalized both capital and labour (Rudolph and Rudolph, 1987). Currently, the neoliberal scholars (e.g. Bhagwati, Srinivasan), whose economically conservative ideas are very powerful and popular now in India, especially, under the tenure of the right-wing government, think that the minimalist state (and absence of regulation of business) will play a developmental role by creating a business-friendly environment (Bhagwati and Panagariya, 2013; Srinivasan, 2011).

In place of these views, I will argue for a class view of the Indian state (Das, 2007), including in its neoliberal form (Das, 2015). Capitalism, along with pre/non-capitalist class relations, define the class context within which the state works. Capitalism is the dominant mode of production in India, and the Indian state is predominantly a capitalist state. The state and capital are two arms of the body of capitalist social relationship (Das, 2017a). The state arm is relatively autonomous of the capital arm, but they are inter-dependent. Subject to the influence of the lower class struggles of workers and peasants (as well as struggles against oppression) combined with the actions and ideologies of state elites and the landed, the two arms affect the conditions under which people, including those who are poor, live. My focus is on the state-arm.

The Indian state is, more or less, moulded by the interests of the coalition of urban capitalists and rural property-owners (large landholders, including those investing in non-farm activities).[2] The state has to protect the property rights of these classes, and their right to buy and sell things as they wish, and their right to exploit[3] the masses whom they employ to produce their wealth. As well, the state generally has to design and implement policies to ensure that the capitalist class can accumulate wealth. Urban capitalists have indeed demanded and benefited, from various state policies. In recent times, cheap sale of state-owned assets (e.g. land; loans) to this class benefits it, while prior to the early 1990s, the state provided infrastructural and capital goods at subsidized prices to business groups that have enriched them.

A specific manifestation of the capitalist class influence on the state is indicated by the fact of financial constraints on the state: these constraints are due to billions of rupees of tax concessions (more than Rs. 36 lakh cores between 2005-06 and 2014-15) (Sainath, 2014) and are due to the fact that billions of rupees have been given to the big business houses by state-owned banks which will never be returned. While the business houses are not paying taxes or not returning loans to state-owned banks, the state has been spending billions to create physical infrastructure (e.g. roads, etc.) in the name of development or vikas, to primarily meet the needs of business houses. All the money that is spent on the wealthy business elite (often on the ground that it will create jobs and make development happen) could be used in the interest of the majority, those who do not have resources to live a decent life. But it cannot be. After spending billions on the elite, the state has been forced to concentrate its resources spatially, leading to regionally uneven development, and to spend an inadequate amount of resources on the poor people.

The other dominant class constitutes approximately the top 10-15 per cent of the rural landholding families. The development of the capitalist elements of this class was in part due to state interventions. These have included: partial implementation of the land reforms that removed some pre-capitalist fetters,[4] and the Green Revolution policy of providing cheap inputs and price support, and the policy of no taxation of rural income. Much of rural capitalism is landlord capitalism. There are also 'pre/non-capitalist' elements in specific regions. The economic dominance of rural landowners is reflected through, and, is reproduced by, the fact that the state considers it legal for them to extract 'pre-capitalist' rent and usurious interest as well as capitalist profit by exploiting rural labour.

Apart from these two ruling classes, state elites as a stratum also benefit from state policies. State elites refer to top bureaucratic and political elites as well as high-level officials who are connected to property-owning classes and who run the public-sector enterprises. State elites exercise power over the millions of poverty-stricken and semi-literate Indians in the name of development and what they increasingly call governance. Yet, state elites are not autonomous of capital. It is the logic of the private sector profit in the hands of the (big) business houses that sets the limit within which specific economic development strategies are designed by state elites, based on their own world-view which is, more or less, influenced by the interests of the bourgeoisie as a whole.[5] The actual nature of policies will depend to some extent on the perception of their own interests and their ideas and the perception of what the nation needs. These include the idea that post-colonial India needs to catch up with the West, the idea about national capitalist development that was relatively autonomous of imperialist pressures, and in more recent times, the elites' penchant for neoliberal ('free-market') development.

The following figure seeks to artistically represent the ways in which dominant classes and state elites influence the state (see the figure below).[6] The Indian state and capital are two arms of the capitalist society. The tail in the picture signifies the feudal and 'semi-feudal' type remnants, whose income/wealth may come from a combination of rent and profit. The state is also enormously influenced by state elites and their attempts to appropriate much of the resources of the state.

The state is also influenced somewhat by the conditions of the life of lower classes, and here it cannot be denied that some powerful state elites (whether from the Right or Centre) have actually wanted to improve the conditions of life of the masses. The state is influenced by the overt/covert struggle of the lower classes against the state and the propertied classes

Figure 6: A Class View of the Indian State

as well. In rural areas lower classes constitute 70 per cent of the rural population. Landowners appropriate surplus labour (or product) from them in the form of rent, interest and profit. As a reserve army of labour—whose size is swelling thanks to neoliberalism (under which there is massive dispossession of small-scale producers from their land)—they are also exploited by urban capitalists in the form of migrant/seasonal labour.

Given the unequal distribution of resources and the attendant exploitative conditions, struggle is immanent. The geography and history of Indian society, like all societies, are the geography and history of class struggle. There is always a potential for struggle even if the potential is not always empirically manifested. Forms of class struggle vary and are often place-specific. The three important forms are: class struggle in the area of production or in the workplace (e.g. struggle against methods and consequences of feudal-type exploitation and capitalist accumulation strategies such as low wages); and, struggle against primitive accumulation (which includes peasants being stripped of their means of production with the aid of the state; privatization of the state's resources). Then there are social struggles or class-relevant struggles including struggles around ecological and gender- and caste-based issues, the struggles in which interests and identities of workers/peasants are not unimportant: oppression based on gender, caste, religion, indigeneity and ecological damage hurt workers and peasants much more than ruling class elements.

Class struggle happens in the context of India's liberal democracy. Indeed, the historical-geographical specificity of India's class society stems partly from the following: unlike most large less-developed countries, India is similar to the countries of the Global North because it has a liberal democracy.[7] India is also quite unlike the northern countries in that the livelihood of a near-majority of its population of 1.25 billion is dependent upon farming, a nature-dependent activity, and that they are deprived of the basic necessities of life such as adequate food, clothing and housing. Given India's size, maintaining territorial and political order amid so much deprivation is a tall order. A liberal democratic capitalist state must not only support accumulation but also legitimize its accumulation policies by giving concessions (anti-poverty policies) and when necessary, use coercion against the lower classes if they resist these policies beyond a certain point.

To conclude the brief conceptual discussion: the Indian state, like any other state, needs to be seen as a dialectical relation between itself and (the class-divided) society. State activity is influenced by its class base. It is also influenced by state-form (federal-democratic form), and by ideas and interests of relatively autonomous state elites. Dominant classes and powerful interests such as those of state elites can condition state action. But they cannot absolutely determine this. Lower class struggles, potential and actual, do influence state policies at different scales and in different places. The fact of the matter is that the class context of the state matters. The history of developmental interventions by the state, especially in rural areas, as discussed below, makes it amply clear that the class context of the state has been a major constraint on its ability to help the poor in any significant sense.

## The Indian State's Developmental Interventions in Rural Areas

### Transformation of Pre-Capitalist Land Relations and Distribution of Land to the Poor (1950s-)

Partly in response to over/covert struggles against unequal land distribution and feudal-type practices and to break class-barriers to capitalist accumulation posed by such practices, the state introduced land reform laws (Das, 1999). These have imposed ceilings (limits) on land ownership, and sought to distribute to poorer people the ceiling-surplus land. Ceilings on landownership in the country were kept at very high levels to protect the landlords' interests.[8] Except in the provinces where there was a strong tradition of the mobilization of the masses by the Left or where there was some geopolitical urgency (as in Kashmir), the state made practically no attempt at locating and distributing the ceiling-surplus land. By 2005, the land distributed to poor people was less than 5 per cent of this potential (and is 1.5 per cent of the total net sown area of the country). Land remains unequally distributed. In 2003, less than 10 per cent of families owned more than 56 per cent of land (Bhalla, 2006: 34). Millions are land-poor or landless.[9] Lack of land, the basic source of subsistence for millions of families, is particularly severe in the case of socially marginalized groups, the Scheduled Castes (SCs) and Scheduled Tribes (STs). Land ownership is a major determinant of income (and power): in the 1990s, someone owning more than 25 acres,[10] earned more than 7.5 times the income of a landless wage earning household (which is approximately Rs. 11,000) (Shariff, 1999: 28).[11]

The land reform laws also aimed at regulating rents and providing tenurial security to tenants. Overwhelmingly dependent on landlords for their living, tenants did not even dare to record their names as tenants (except in Bengal), and hence could not seek protection from the new laws. Even those registered as tenants could not afford the money necessary to fight a case and wait indefinitely for the judgment. Nor did they have the money to buy the land by paying compensation to the landlords.

## Promotion of Technological Change in the Food Sector (1960s-)

Following the failure of the land reform measures, which were expected to increase land productivity by protecting small-scale peasant farming and providing tenurial security and thus to expand the domestic market, the state launched a second rural development policy, the Green Revolution, in the late 1960s. This policy aimed at increased food production through technological change and specifically the use of high-yielding seeds. There was some improvement in farm productivity and profitability. Associated with this, the relations of production, or class relations, changed in two ways. Attracted by greater profitability, in many areas, landlords evicted their tenants and started direct cultivation by using hired workers, some of whom were erstwhile tenants. Initially, labourers obtained some employment at increased wages, but a subsequent increase in the use of machinery by the employers (and their deployment of migrant workers from areas outside the Green Revolution areas), threatened to displace a large number of agricultural workers and slowed down/stopped the tendency towards any gain in wages. The state did not do much to ensure that landowners pay workers an adequate living wage. Thus market-oriented, profit driven, cultivation was given a boost. So while landowners gained, workers did not benefit as much.

The technology itself was expensive. It was generally monopolized by larger land-owners of relative higher castes, who control local state apparatuses that provide credit and/or subsidized inputs. So, smaller owners, who could not invest as much as larger owners did not benefit much. Many leased out their land to larger owners because they could not profitably invest in the technology. This was the case even though the Green Revolution resulted in an overall increase in yields. Poorer peasants and tribals, who had less land or no land and who had limited access to credit, did not benefit much.

Finally, the benefits from the Green Revolution technology were geographically concentrated as a result of a deliberate strategy by the state to concentrate resources in specially endowed areas (e.g. areas with irrigation facilities) to get quick results (Shiva, 1991). This meant that vast areas remained deprived of public investment, resulting in a low level of technological change and high level of poverty. In fact, as mentioned earlier, such spatial inequality prompted migration of landless workers and poor peasants from economically backward areas to the Green Revolution areas, and this allowed capitalist farmers in the latter areas to pay lower wages, including to local workers. Thus inequality between areas has had an effect on class inequality.

## Provision of Cheap Credit to the Poor (1970s-)

As the Green Revolution could not significantly reduce poverty, in the late 1970s, the state launched the Integrated Rural Development Policy (IRDP). This aimed at giving small loans to poor people to start income-generating activities—setting up small shops, starting dairy businesses, using improved farm equipment, etc. This policy, more or less, was also a failure. The amount of assistance allocated per person was limited. The limited money that the state could commit did not even reach the intended beneficiaries. Officials and politicians worked in an utterly undemocratic manner and had unscrupulous links to traders. Therefore, much of the IRDP money ended up in the pockets of the local officials, or with the traders supplying the assets needed for the income-generating activities (e.g. animals; farm implements) (Das, 2000). Given a choice between converting a meagre state loan to 'capital' and using it to buy food, they would just choose the latter. This they did. The fact that it is difficult for starving poor people to be profit-earning entrepreneurs and to generate enough income which would lift them out of poverty on a sustainable basis and on a mass scale, this very fact, did not occur to the apologists of capital and World Bankish people who were, and are, hawkishly eager to promote market relations in every nook and corner of the country and the world.

### Creation of Wage-Employment Through Public Works (2006-)

Partly due to the pressure from the Left and progressive forces, the state started (somewhat reluctantly), in 2006, a new policy of employment creation, known as the National Rural Employment Guarantee Scheme or NREGS. Its aim is to provide at least 100 days of guaranteed waged employment a year to every household whose adult members volunteer to do unskilled manual work at the legislated minimum wage. Reports suggest that, like the IRDP, a large part of the money meant for this policy has gone to the politicians, officials and property-owners (e.g. contractors), except in those few areas where the poor people are able to exercise constant vigilance over the implementation of the scheme (Khera, 2008; Liberation, 2008; Rai, 2007). Provisions of the Act are routinely violated. For example, the delay in the payment of wages lasts for weeks and months; labourers are not paid the unemployment insurance if they are not provided wage-work when they demand. There is also not enough money provided for the policy to work (to give everyone wage work at a decent living wage as and when they need it). In recent years, the allocation for the programme has shrunk, including under the current right-wing regime.

## Why Has the State Failed to Significantly Improve the Conditions of the Poor-Majority?

### Dominant Classes

Contrary to the perception of poverty alleviation, a perception manufactured through faulty unrealistic statistical definition of poverty, it is the case that the major interventions of the post-colonial state have failed to significantly improve the conditions of life of the poor, the conditions that are created by the ways in which the capitalist economic-political system works. The main, if not the sole, reason for state failure is the class character of the state and society. As in other similar post-colonial countries, large landowners in India share state power with the urban bourgeoisie: this means that state policies have been dominantly in the interests of these classes and their international patrons. The landowners[12] perform the important role of economically and politically controlling the rural masses, including labourers, whose anger against landlordism could be potentially directed at the bourgeoisie of the country as well as their international patrons. Further, those who are responsible for the design and implementation of pro-poor policies, for monitoring their progress, and for managing the (angry) response of the poor to the non-performance of the policies—and they include civil servants, judges, the police and state-supported intellectual elites—come from the landed class or represented their interests.[13]

The class interest of the landed was in the ruthless exploitation of people with little or no land: as poor peasants, who are subjected to rental extractions and who are (increasingly) working as labourers at below-subsistence wages, often under unfree conditions. Heavy rental extraction meant that peasants had insufficient resources to invest in land. Super exploitation of peasants and labourers also reduced the size of the home market. Besides, given the opportunity to earn revenue through these means of super-exploitation, property owners had scarcely any incentive to invest in land to increase labour productivity. Thus, to the extent that one can at all isolate national-scale factors of under-development from imperialism, defined specifically "as a form of class relations: relations between metropolitan bourgeoisie and Third World workers/peasants" (Das, 2001b: 168), agrarian class relations acted as a fetter on the development of productive forces, at least in specific regions. This contradicted capitalists' interests in a) higher rates of profit which would have come from cheaper farm products for food and raw materials and b) a growing home market allowing large-scale production. So, landowners were potential enemies of the urban capitalist class. The economic interest of the capitalist class, domestic and foreign, was such that it would not have had any problem if the land reform legislation had completely destroyed the pre-capitalist class. Such legislation would also have improved the material conditions of peasants and rural labourers. But the political interests of capitalists were such that they could not go against the feudals. What Marx said in 1852 (in a chapter in the *New York Daily Tribune*) about the then-British bourgeoisie, is relevant to their Indian counterpart now: "They prefer to compromise with the vanishing opponent [i.e. the feudals] rather than to strengthen the arising enemy [i.e. the working class], to whom the future belongs, by concessions of a more than apparent importance. Therefore, they strive to avoid every forcible collision with [them]' (Marx, 2000: 361). So, given the importance of the landowners, the state acting on behalf of the bourgeoisie could not afford to hurt their (i.e. landowners') interest too much by properly implementing land reforms.

The Green Revolution, in a sense, represented a continuity with the earlier programme (i.e. the land reforms), once again revealing the class character of the state. The Green Revolution policy placed new means of production (e.g. the new technological package; state capital in the form of subsidized loans, etc.) precisely in the hands of the same class which was protected by the land reforms policy, and allowed it an opportunity to accumulate capital, unfettered and untaxed. They continue to govern the conditions of existence of the poor.[14] Neither the land-reforms nor the Green Revolution did anything to significantly undermine the economic and political power of large property owners (many of whom also invested in non-farm activities such as transportation, trading, etc.). I may add that in the post-Green Revolution era, and especially, since the onset of neoliberal capitalist policies, India's land and water resources are increasingly being used to produce high value goods for a narrow domestic elite and for export.[15] And one implication of this is a relative decline in per capita food production, as widely reported in the works of Utsa Patnaik (see Figure 7 below which traces changes in per capita foodgrain output during the colonial and post-colonial times).

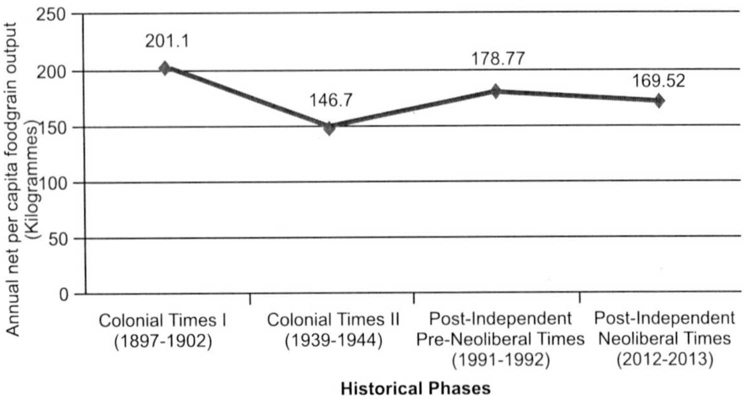


Figure 7: Changes in Per Capita Food Grain Output in India: Colonial and Post-Independent

Also, another new, post-1990s, tendency is that the method of technological upgrading of the rural sector has been in the form of contract farming, which is a form of corporate control over farming which is bound to have adverse consequences for peasants and labourers (see Shrimali, 2015 for an excellent discussion on this).

Given the overall capitalist class context, the amount of funding for the proper implementation of the policies on the scale that is necessary has to be necessarily limited. In the market system, the use of society's resources must be justified mainly on the basis of the profit-logic. This logic has put severe limits on the amount of money the capitalist state could commit in the form of pro-poor policies, such as the IRDP (or universal public distribution system), relative to the massive need of the hundreds of millions of the poor whom the system marginalizes (e.g. peasants increasingly losing access to land; people without secure employment with a living wage). The actual amount spent on the poor depends on, among other things, the balance of class forces as mediated by political-administrative mechanisms (e.g. judiciary, electoral power, etc.), and this balance is, generally, not in favour of the nation's poor, even if the balance of power may be slightly more in their favour in some regions than in others. But there are severe structural limits to what the state can do for the poor.[16] Note that these limits are expressed by the ruling class, directly or through its spokespersons, who have no qualms about milking the state to satisfy their appetite for profits. The situation of state spending for the poor relative to the country's ability to spend is stark in the post-1991 period. One of the (contradictory) aims of the latter is to shrink mass income and consumption at home in order to, for example, enable cheap exports and repayment of debt to imperialist finance capital (see Patnaik, 1999).[17] Since the inception of neoliberalism, rural development expenditures, as a ratio of the net national product, have dropped from 2.8 per cent in 1993-94 to 2.6 per cent in 1995-96 to 1.9 per cent in 2000-01 (Patnaik, 2007: 155). Among other things, this has led to a reduction in the creation of employment opportunities.[18]

Given that the state must protect economic and political interests of the large property owning families, the daily activities of the state must be insulated from the constant democratic monitoring of it by the masses. But without their popular participation in the everyday workings of the state, including the ways in which pro-poor policies are implemented, government funds meant for the poor are squeezed on their way from the national and provincial-level state apparatuses, to the local-level government officials/politicians.[19] This explains why landowners can hide their land, why they can monopolize Green Revolution technology and get away with the non-payment of minimum wages, why the money meant for the poor in the form of anti-poverty policies ends up reaching the pockets of the rural rich and government politicians and officials (Das, 1999; 2000).

When viewed in relation to policies for the lower classes/castes, the Indian state is a deeply contradictory entity. On the one hand, without the democratic grassroots organization of these classes vis-a-vis economic elites and the state elites, these policies will fail. On the other hand, its own actions and ideas and its own form (liberal electoral democracy), the form of anti-poverty policies, whether Land Reforms or other policies, tend to fragment and disorganize the lower classes/castes who compete for meagre resources (indeed government spending for the poor is decreasing). Not only must it disorganize, it must also have a certain amount of social-political distance between itself and the lower classes. Indeed, real direct democratic control over the state's day-to-day operation by the lower classes contradicts the state's function to reproduce class relations. In its day-to-day operation, the state is generally not accessible to lower classes the way it is to dominant classes. Therefore, state officials properly implementing anti-poverty policies does not generally arise. If lack of power contributes to poverty, the state is a cause of powerlessness of the lower classes. It must therefore be seen as an important cause of poverty. We should be critical of those who are sanguine about the talk of decentralization of state power as a solution to problems.

## Conclusion

So what is to be done to resolve this contradiction, i.e. to address the massive persistent poverty problem? The poor people—i.e. the lower classes (proletarians and semi-proletarians and petty-producers)—must make a democratic demand on the state around radical needs. Radical needs are the real needs of the masses, not the needs which the system says it can afford to meet. This is, for a start, about the redefinition of poverty. Poverty should not be about not having Rs. 32 or Rs. 47 a day. To solve the problem of poverty is much more than reducing hunger. The reality of poverty should not be conflated with the misperception of the governmental elite about what the poor need, nor should it be a matter of what the misleaders of the people parrot or repeat about vikas at election rallies.

The poor should democratically organize themselves over multiple 'rights' reflecting their needs: right to employment (including the right to more land and other farm inputs for poor peasants in agrarian economies), a living wage, a reduced working day and leisure, decent and affordable housing, high-quality healthcare and education as well as culture.[20] These rights also include the right to decent financial support for the elderly and the disabled and for low-income women needing maternity benefits, and the right to a healthy and safe environment at work and in neighbourhoods. Those who have small amounts of land must have access to land, and state-provision of means of production, complete freedom from landlord, usurious and mercantile exploitation.

The poor must fight for the defence of democratic rights, including those of aboriginal populations, religious minorities and low castes. This is especially important in the current times when a Hindu-nationalist right-wing regime, representing the interests of large sections of the property-owning class and continuing the economic policies of the 'centrist' Congress regime with a greater commitment to markets, divides the masses by using religion (Hindus vs non-Hindus). It is thus able to implement blatantly pro-business policies by weakening any potential/real opposition and by popularizing a notion of the homogeneous nation (a Hindu nation) in the interest of which all opposition to pro-business and undemocratic policies must be curtailed. Such a regime also sells the idea of development or vikas (read free-market economic growth meaning accumulation of profit) and throws some crumbs at the poor, to capture governmental power and then makes use of this power to crush democratic rights of minorities. The demand for the protection of democratic rights of minorities is in the interest of the bloc of the lower classes (proletarians, semi-proletarians and small-scale self-employed producers) as a whole.

The poor must put the agenda of their democratic control over landed and financial aristocrats and over capitalist monopolies as immediate steps necessary to satisfy their social needs. This agenda is particularly important when it comes to those monopolies which control the production of things and services (e.g. food items and seeds, medicines, houses, clothes, utilities, etc.) without which radical needs cannot be met and people cannot live like humans. It is clear that the poor masses cannot rely on the bourgeoisie and its state nor on the non-militant, Left forces who spend their energies mainly on electoral battles, to resolve the democratic and agrarian questions in the interest of the poor.

In other words, the poor people must reimagine democracy: democracy is much more than being able to vote for this or that person or party once every few years. It must be about the control over the ways society's resources are used and over the ways in which the state institutions work and meet the economic and political needs of the poor. Therefore, the preparatory step towards a permanent solution to the problem of poverty requires deepening India's democratic tradition, as a part of a similar global democratizing process. The poor as well as those who speak on their behalf must re-imagine democracy as it originally was and as it should be: the democracy of the poor, the majority.

## Notes

1. By the state, I refer to the structure of institutions of domination, including government, the army, police, and the executive.
2. In this coalition, dominant are the urban capitalists—especially the larger owners of capital with national and, under the current neoliberal dispensation, international, scale of operations.
3. The capitalist class exploits in the sense that it pays a wage to its workers so the latter can live a normal life and are able to continue to work but the workers produce for the capitalist class a lot more than they receive in wages. The masses are over-exploited when the wage falls short of what is needed for a normal life. The state in India has overseen both the system of exploitation and over-exploitation.
4. Economic development under capitalist social relations usually requires destruction of pre-capitalist property relations. But the state failed to fully break the monopoly of the landed. This led to constricted demand for industrial goods.
5. This does not mean that every policy of the state perfectly attends to the interest of all capitalists. Different capitalists have different interests. Personal and institutional connection between state elites and business houses may also produce policies that may not exactly benefit the entire capitalist class at a given point in time. State elites also need to be mindful of public order: i.e. potential resistance to pro-business policies from lower classes (see below), and this consideration influences policies that may not immediately meet capitalist economic interests. Generally, over the long run, state policies tend to support capitalist class interests and especially, interests of the dominant sections.

6. This figure was constructed by a former doctoral student of mine, Rajiv Rawat, based on my initial drawing.
7. That there has been an ongoing attack on it in recent times is a separate matter.
8. For example, the ceiling for a family in Andhra Pradesh was 877 acres. Ceilings were lowered in the 1970s in part as a response to agrarian struggles.
9. Owners with more than 10 acres own 34.63 per cent of the land and account for 12.78 per cent of rural households including the landless, while the number of landless households, or families who were near-landless (owning less than 5 acres) constitute 90.4 per cent of rural households in 2003 (Bhalla, 2007).
10. This person is likely to obtain most of his/her income in the form of rent from tenants and/or profit from daily-wage labourers.
11. I fully accept Mr. Sudhir Patnaik's friendly criticism following my Utkal University lecture on January 7, 2017, that I miss the fact that a large amount of land is in the hands of the state itself and that this has not been distributed among the poor but could be. The movement for more equal distribution of land, a process that would contribute to democratization of social relations, must encompass state land as well as privately-held land.
12. They include the pre-capitalist elements of this class (e.g. former rajas, zamindars, etc who were supporters of imperialism) were powerful in specific regions.
13. If large landowners' farms were broken and their land was consequently redistributed among poorer peasants and the landless, and if the latter were provided technological and financial support by the state through cooperatives, land productivity would have increased, putting money in their hands and creating a home market. This did not happen. This could not happen. This is because of the overall balance of class forces, within the country and internationally (i.e. influence of imperialists).
14. That radicals had expected otherwise (that bureaucratic land reforms would be progressive and that the Green Revolution would bring about technological change, and empower poorer peasants with proper state support), without any radical change in the balance of class forces, signifies their fascination with the national progressive bourgeois thesis and the idea that the nation-state in an imperialized country can help bring about radical long-term rural transformation in property relations and expand the productive forces.
15. Under the current neoliberal-capitalist regime, the legal restriction on land ownership is considered by domestic and foreign capital and their political and ideological supporters to be an institutional constraint on the flow of agribusiness investment to rural areas of the country. That is why the existing ceiling on land is being relaxed as it is seen as a

constraint on acquiring agricultural, homestead and forestlands for a variety of agricultural as well as non-agricultural purposes including export-oriented capitalist industrialization (Special Economic Zones or SEZs) (Pushpendra, 2000).

16. These are ideologically expressed through such constructs as 'budget deficits go up' or 'government assistance makes people lazy' or that 'people should take initiatives to solve their problems'.
17. Shrinking income and consumption of the toiling classes is the characteristic aspect of neoliberalism everywhere (including in imperialist countries), not just in peripheral countries. This means that there is a potential basis for international solidarity of working class and small-scale self-employed producers against capital, including its neoliberal avatar, everywhere and at all scales.
18. The limited help available from the government in the name of the economic reforms with a human face has not been enough to counter the inhumane effects of neoliberalism (on rural income, employment and access to land).
19. Like landlords, government officials and politicians are utterly insensitive to the problems of the poor, as even liberal scholars recognize (see Subramanian, 1998).
20. This includes access to films, television programmes, music, museums, and the like that are not controlled by big business and its politicians.

# 10

# Developmental Crisis and Politics of Protest Against Neoliberalism

The crisis talk is ubiquitous. We are living in an age of crisis. There is a global financial crisis. We were told it was over. But it seems another one is on the horizon. In poor countries such as India, there is an agrarian crisis. Some scholars (e.g. Patnaik) are even talking about the agrarian root of the global crisis while others (e.g. Harvey) talk about its urban root. One can also talk about a crisis of development.

The development crisis—connected as it is to the agrarian crisis—is interesting. It means, among other things, that people cannot simply survive as they have in the past. Many of them are failing to keep their small asset-base intact, slowly selling their tangible resources (e.g. land, cattle, etc.): simple reproduction is becoming difficult. Worse, millions are failing to reproduce themselves and their future generation at the current level (or as they have in the recent past), as the brilliant empirical work of P. Sainath, Utsa Patnaik and others has been reminding us. Many people are simply dying prematurely due to hunger or semi-hunger conditions: they die due to illnesses caused by material deprivation of various forms. Thousands are just giving up living because they cannot carry on living like sub-humans. Many 'semi-conscious' bearers of the system—including educated people managing it—often explain starvation-induced illness/death in terms of the absence of knowledge (or in terms of incorrect knowledge) on the part of the dead: that is, they do not possess the knowledge about how to eat and live. Animals in imperialist countries are fed much better than millions of people in poor countries such as India. Animals earn a lot more (subsidies) from the system than millions of humans in our world.

Ideas do not create the current material reality in any straightforward, immediate sense. But a set of ideas can act like a material force, when many people believe in these. An aspect of the development crisis is, to some extent, a crisis at the level of ideas. This crisis is the collective failure among the progressives to rigorously theorize social relations of development itself with an emancipatory content and intent. Is the development crisis due to a democratic deficit, due to an undemocratic relationship between the governed and those who govern, a non-transparent relationship between the state and its (poorer) citizens? Is it due to remnants of a feudal-type, caste-based and patriarchal practices? Is it because of the profit-driven system operating at the national and international scales? Is the development crisis happening because imperialism is crushing the social and economic 'rights' of the masses? If all these are true, how are they interconnected? Or, are they? What is the main contradiction underlying the development crisis? At what geographical scale should the main contradiction be theorized: local, regional, national or international, or all of these? Is it possible to resolve fully the non-main contradictions without beginning to attack the main contradiction? We are failing to adequately and dialectically think about all this.

## Necessity for the Fight for Reforms, and its Limited Nature

This sort of intellectual failure is associated with a political failure in some circles. Many people—including sections of the urban youth—want to change things. But this wanting is often, more or less, limited to 'protest politics' against the 'excesses'[1] of the system: against this or that unfair policy of the government, this or that case of corruption, against cases of dispossession here and there (e.g. the campaigns against 'the

Poscos'). The quality of democracy would be poorer without these protests. These protests are necessary. Social theoretically, these suggest, as Anthony Giddens once remarked, that humans will always resist oppression unless they are drunk. But there is little indication that these protests are being seen, in theory and practice, as parts of a system of political-intellectual campaigns against a common, or the central, target (i.e. use of society's resources for limitless private gain and exploitation of labour). There is also not much indication that the 'ubiquitous' protest politics is guided by any notion of radical demands: demanding the totality of all the things that we need (adequate food, shelter, education, healthcare, culture, democratic accountability, political and intellectual freedom, sustainable environment, etc.). These are the things we need in order to live like humans and we need these things now. What the paid political-intellectual managers of the system think in terms of what we need and can get should not affect our conception of what we need. What we need is given by the materiality[2] of our body, by the social conditions of our living including the level of productive forces, culture, etc.

As stressed in a previous Chapter, there is a need for an intransigent theory that lays bare the unbending and unyielding character of the current system of economic and political power relations and at the same time charts the possibilities of reforms, within the framework of a project of transcending the system that is driven by the endless pursuit of profit while the basic needs of the vast majority remain unmet. It must recognize this: concessions are possible to obtain but seen in a proper time-space perspective, every little concession given here and now is taken back—or can be taken back—there or in another point of time, unless the masses control political power (i.e. state power), and society's control over resources. The temporal and spatial life of the system is much larger than individuals' and groups' indeed. The intransigent theory must also recognize that every material concession is used ideologically to produce consent in the minds of people to the system, consent to the idea that 'the system can be reformed, so please be patient'.[3] Notice the contradiction: the system teaches patience, but it itself is based on an incessant process of money-making. We are told that we need to sacrifice our current satisfaction of needs at the altar of the profit-driven market system which will deliver good things in the future. The system is bathed with a passion, the passion for wealth in the abstract and the passion to crush any fundamental opposition to it. It is permeated with 'revolutionary' impatience, impatient to make as much money (even illegally) briefly as possible. But there does not appear to be a corresponding revolutionary impatience or urgency or passion on the part of the oppressed, or on the part of their organic intellectuals and political leaders.[4] In other words: the system (ruled by the 1-10 per cent) is impatient, but the bottom 90-99 per cent does not appear to be so (or its impatience is sought to be disciplined both by 'protest politicians' who often direct, intentionally or not, the masses' anger into safe channels, and by coercive organs of the state). Underlying the contradiction mentioned above is a deep hiatus between the system's concept of time and that of the oppressed. For the system (or, more correctly, the 1-10 per cent which rules it): things have to happen quickly, money has to be made quickly, 'labour reforms' will have to be passed quickly which will allow companies to fire employees freely, etc. For those living at the bottom, the idea, more or less, is 'postponism': that we can wait to be fed better; that we can wait to see a completely new world, and that all we can do now is to ask for some reforms. Notice also another contradiction: between greed of the top strata and asceticism of the bottom. The top seeks to make as much money as it can and satisfy its most diverse needs for luxuries. And the bottom has to be satisfied with less, with small concessions.

The post-ponism of the majority and its asceticism are not unconnected with how those who seek to speak on behalf of the majority and in their interest theorize the system, in terms of what is the main contradiction underlying the various forms of the crisis of development. Underlying the belief that we can fight for a change here and there is a deeply philosophical inclination towards a combination of empiricism, presentism and reformism/opportunism: visible evidence of some concession here, at the present moment, is used to theoretically mean that the system can deliver significant concessions always: what we see—the system being able to deliver some concessions, some progressive legislation—is mistakenly taken by many to be what is real, i.e. what is fundamentally true about the system. The durability of the system—its naturalization—is enormously helped by this kind of thinking, which, ontologically, reduces what is real to what appears to be real.

Underlying many of the campaigns (protest political activities) is this belief in the potential reformability of the system for the good of all in the long run. We forget that: when, for example, a wage increase is won in one place in a province or the country, it may come at the expense of a fund to pay for maternity leave or workplace safety or workers' wages of workers not going on a strike in another place, or it may come at the expense of workers' solidarity in situ (a slight wage increase can be granted on the ground that workers will not go on a strike or form an independent union). A theory of wage cannot rule out wage increase. Even when wage increase happens on a larger scale than in a few companies or locally, i.e. even if it happens, say, nationally, we must understand two things. One is this that, as Marx remarks in *Capital* Vol. 1 (Ch. 25), even if wages increase, it only means that the length and weight of the golden chain around the wage-worker is somewhat loosened, and that we reproduce ourselves as slightly better-fed slaves for the property owners. The increase in wages can never be allowed to threaten the system itself. The structural character of the system sets the limit on how good our life can be, as individuals or groups of individuals. As soon as the rise in wages interferes with the normal rate of profit making, wages start falling. After winning some wage increase due to both favourable circumstances of accumulation and a certain degree of unionization, American workers in the auto-industry are now forced to sell themselves for almost half the wage they used to receive.

What is needed is a theory that is systemic and multi-scalar. This theory must recognize what is present (e.g. class exploitation, imperialism, national and social oppression, profit-driven ecological destruction, gross commercialization of all spheres of human life including culture and social relations) ontologically at various levels (i.e. levels of structural mechanisms and empirical events. Only this sort of recognition of the present can escape from empiricism (the idea that only what is seen/measured is real). This theory must also recognize what is absent (e.g. collective democratic control over our lives, our planet, our bodies, our destiny, our culture). The theory must acknowledge explanatorily that what is present is the main cause of what is absent. So the theory must be critical of the present. And the theory must therefore recognize politically that what is 'absent' has to be presented and what is present has to be absented and point to what is to be done. And this theorization has to be performed at multiple scales, and most specifically, nationally and internationally, and with a sensitivity towards the longer time scale at which the system's tendencies, and mechanisms, operate. Is there a whole lot in between these absenting and presenting practices, in the longer term? Dialectically seen, has humanity created a possibility for anything really significant between individualist control and collective control, between making money for the sake of money (even fictitious money) and the satisfaction of democratically-defined human needs? No.

The fight for concessions—including democratization of the government—is enormously worth it. It is worthwhile, especially if it increases the fighting power of the poor-majority for the ultimate absenting of the present. Surely, someone who has not eaten for days cannot be expected to fight against a law that bans abortion rights or the right to form a union. Immediate relief is important. Concessions are also worth fighting for if the process of fighting inculcates an awareness among the masses that there are strong limits to what is possible to gain within the system and if they teach the masses the political and intellectual skills necessary to fight (and to manage a different future world).[5] Intellectually, progressives can assess the significance of the fight for reforms on these (and perhaps other similar) grounds. Politically, they can encourage reforms on these and other similar grounds.[6] But these intellectual and political tasks presuppose the following recognition: the need for the fight for concessions in/from the system is informed by a proper theory of the system itself. To theorize the system is to unpack its logic of operation, the mechanisms and tendencies. And the fight for reforms must be a part of a wider fight, based on the lessons learnt from the fight for reforms, to replace the existing system. The fight for reforms must be based on the recognition that significant reforms can generally come only when there is a palpable threat at home or abroad to the existence of the system itself, of property relations and to the state which protects these.

We should remember that we live in a world where wealth is produced for money making, where we will feed ourselves as long as we feed the system with money, where we work as long as we live and live as long as we work. In the current arrangements, our everyday activities as a species are not directly geared towards the satisfaction of our manifold needs as humans. Therefore, when concessions are given, it is not necessarily because the system wants to satisfy our needs. Much rather it is because, as just mentioned, the system is somewhat fearful of the masses (turning more revolutionary). Sometimes even the ultra-rich can ask to be taxed a little, or taxed slightly more than they usually are, or they ask for being regulated a little by the government (in fact, arguments for limited reduction in inequality come from them and their spokespersons). All this self-abnegation happens purely because of their fear of possible 'negation of negation' (expropriation of the expropriators). This temporary self-denial on the part of the ruling elite happens because of their anxiety about their future, not about ours.[7] In other words, concessions are given by the elite to keep the system going so that the product of our work and our property based on our own earnings (self-earned private property such as land, of peasants) can continue to be taken away from us. Concession-giving is really the opposite of what it appears to be. It is not giving. It is taking. Everything stands on its head in this modern class-divided world, which has an enormous capacity to create false ideas in our minds. Concessions are a small part of the system. The system determines—sets limit on—the manner, the form, the magnitude, the timing and spacing of the concessions. Concessions are not an indicator of the goodness or legitimacy of the system. A few benefits wrung from the system do not change much the fundamental character of the system, any more than a few pieces of falling hair make a person bald. Such is the law of quantity and quality in dialectics. And there have been fewer and fewer of these benefits anyway in the recent past.

## Struggle Against Industrialization

In this section, I wish to reflect on, in the light of the general points made thus far, on the struggles against industrialization that are occurring in different parts of India. Industrialization is understood narrowly in the sense of manufacturing and broadly in the sense of the application of modern science and technology to the transformation of raw materials from nature. It is necessary for national development, as the economist Gavin Kitching and others argued decades ago. Industrialization adds value to unprocessed goods extracted from nature and thus increases society's income. Often owners of land (peasants) do not earn more, or do not earn much more than, those who work in industry as wage labourers. Industrialization makes possible the production of a vast range of goods, which are directly used by people: clothes, materials required to build houses, traditional and Western medicines, consumer durables, cultural items such as books and musical instruments; the different types of food that go through the manufacturing process, etc. And, industry indeed produces the means of production necessary in both farming and industry itself. Industrialization holds out the possibility of ending want and material suffering. It provides employment to the increasing population, including through forward and backward linkages. It makes it possible to reap scale economies and specialization in ways not possible in agriculture. In part because of the above, industrialization increases labour productivity, one of the fundamental indicators of progress, prosperity, and economic development in the society at large. Industrialization breaks the mutual isolation of producers: this happens as they now work in great numbers in large cities and towns. Their geographical concentration will potentially allow them to fight for justice and equality in society, both on their behalf and on behalf of other oppressed groups. Industrialization, connected as it is to science, promotes a culture of rational thinking and can potentially undermine the basis for superstitious and obscurantist ideas and practices. Given these and many other advantages of industrialization, the Left—at least, the Marxist Left—cannot be opposed to industrialization (although sections of the postmodern/populist Left are, as industrialization is seen by them as a sign/carrier of modernity that supposedly destroys an authentic pre-modern culture). The question is: what form of industrialization should the Left endorse in theory and practice? What happens when, for example, a proposed SEZ (special economic zone) displaces thousands of peasants? Should industrialization be endorsed under this situation?

To answer this question, one may start with agriculture. Land is the most important means of production in agriculture, at least at the current stage when farming is relatively less capital-intensive. Fertility of land is a product of natural forces as well as human investments. It is normally the case that human investments in land to raise land fertility happen closer to existing centres of population and commerce than away from these. Fertile tracts of land therefore are generally located closer to existing centres of population and commerce. Now, owners of industry also need land. But their need for land is different. They need to locate their factories on: land is not used as an input in the way it is used in farming. And in a market economy, they need land in a specific location: industry tends to be located closer to existing centres of population and commerce for the reason that greater profits are made possible by greater geographical accessibility. Therefore, the fight over industrialization often becomes a fight between owners of industry and owners of land (including peasants). This fight is over not just an absolute piece of land but over its location.

To be able to understand the ongoing struggles over industrialization, we have to carefully distinguish between industrialization per se which is necessary in all modern societies from its various historically specific forms, and we need to also distinguish between various forms of struggle over industrialization.

There is a strong logic to locating industry on the land which is not currently cultivated or irregularly cultivated, in relatively less accessible locations and away from the locations of fertile land on which peasants are currently dependent on or which may soon be used. Why? Firstly, as mentioned above, industry does not need fertile land as an input. Location of a factory on or close to a fertile land destroys natural fertility of soil which is almost impossible to manufacture in industry. It is indeed a great social cost to use a fertile land for industrialization which does not need it. Secondly, forcing the industry to locate in these areas (e.g. relatively less accessible areas, away from fertile land) will result in the development of new means of transportation and communication (which will also create jobs). Industrialization in these less accessible locations will also give an impetus to agriculture in places around it. This would contribute to the integrated coexistence of farming and industrial activity in a region and to the undermining of the rural-urban divide. It is unfortunate that when industries could be located in more remote locations on land that is relatively less fertile, they are being located on currently cultivated fertile land. This must be fought against. This is one form of the struggle over industrialization.

If, however, a fertile land currently being cultivated must absolutely be used for an SEZ—and whether this must be the case should be democratically decided and not decided by business—several conditions must be laid out. The value of the land as a compensation to the family must be determined in relation to what the value of the land would be after the industries have come up. Under no circumstances must the living standards of the families losing the land and the families losing access to employment on that land (farm labourers, tenants) be allowed to be worse than what they were before the change in the use of the land. Indeed, because industrialization will make possible greater production of wealth and because this is possible only by displacing the people who currently occupy the land and depend on its use, it must be an absolute precondition of displacement that their material and cultural needs (adequate food, clothes, shelter, education, healthcare, etc.) are satisfied (including by giving permanent employment in the industry to at least one person from every affected family with a living wage and retirement benefits) and that environmental sustainability of the place and nearby-places is maintained. Investment must be made in the lives of the people who are affected before the investment is made in the SEZ itself. This will not happen automatically since it requires a democratically mobilized struggle. This is the second form of struggle over industrialization.

Peasants as peasants have been involved in heroic battles over dispossession from their land—in Bengal, in northern Orissa, in Maharashtra, and so many other places. This is not the decisive battle against the industrialist class (domestic or foreign), however. The decisive battle against it cannot be, and will not be, fought by peasants as property owners against dispossession, although local and temporary success is possible. The battle against unjust dispossession—capitalists' right to dispossess, the right which serves their interest and not the dispossessed—can only be successfully fought by an alliance of urban workers, peasants and rural workers. That such an alliance is developing is an interesting development.[8]

Note also that the issue of peasants being separated from land is not a single act of a group of industrialists, backed by the state, an act that can be isolated from other things happening that affect the peasants (and workers). Let me explain. Given high costs of farm inputs which come from the industry and given the decreasing prices of farm products from which industry benefits, millions of peasants, including rich peasants, are going into debt. To clear their debt, they are selling their land (or when farming is not paying, they are enticed to offer the sale of their lands). Many are leasing their land to better-off farmers, including those who enter into contract with industrialists, domestic and foreign, to produce farm products for industrial processing, and this signifies a form of separation from land (operational land, if not ownership land). There is, therefore, a potential site of struggle against this insidious form of dispossession from—and loss of control over—land, as a part of the wider process of class differentiation. There is an additional fact to consider: given the vast mass of unemployed and under-employed people in the cities, industrialists are able to make one person do the work of, say, two, and this reduces further demand for labour, which means that even if peasants do not wish to do farming, they are forced to engage in farming, which does not pay. So super-exploitation of urban labour, which may even include family members of peasants, living/working in the village, directly affects the peasants, and that should be a target of struggle.

Such struggle against exploitation of labour must happen inside SEZs. Peasants turned into the proletariat in the SEZs, in newly industrializing areas—whether located on fertile land, displacing peasants or in remote locations—will and must fight against the monied class, initially for better wages and working conditions. One may respond by saying that the SEZ framework of industrialization does not allow for the working class organization. But then who said that the SEZ must be a necessary form of industrialization? Or if it does, who said that an SEZ—understood as an industrial cluster—must be one where workers are to be alienated from their democratic right to organize? If business has the right to make money, then should workers not have the right to organize, to demand a decent life? This is an additional form of struggle over industrialization, the struggle that connects workers of different industrial clusters and cities politically and that demands that industrialization must be of a particular form such that those who do the work must be fully able to meet their social and cultural needs.

An SEZ, an industrial project, of course, involves separating people from their land, and often forcible separation. An SEZ is also based on the fact that the worker gets only a small part of what he/she produces for capitalists. The SEZ represents endless money-making at one pole and limitless misery at another. This form of industrialization does not just produce things that are of potential use. It reproduces an invisible relation of separation of masses from their lives, a relation between them and those who control their lives at work (and outside). So because separation of people from their property (land, etc.) creates a ground for the second form of separation (i.e. separation of workers from the fruits of their labour in the workplace),[9] the struggle against the former must be connected to the struggle over the latter, and can only be fully successful if it is connected that way.

Protecting the peasants does not necessarily mean protecting the peasant property. If industrialization can improve the conditions of peasants (i.e. outside of farming), perhaps 'sacrificing' their property to make room for industrialization, if peasants so desire, can be favourably considered. Everyone must be provided with an opportunity to live a life with dignity. Whether it is in industry or farming should, ordinarily, be beside the matter. But there is an 'if', as in 'If industrialization can better conditions of life of peasants...' and if peasants voluntarily wish to leave farming and give up their ownership of land. Industrialization, whether led by state-capital or private capital has not done much for millions of peasants. And it will not unless it is a site of class-contestation.

## Conclusion

There are different dimensions of how the system works in relation to peasants. And this points to an important conclusion about capitalists: the industrialists, who set up an SEZ by displacing peasants from land, the industrialists who benefit from high prices of industrial goods (farm inputs) sold to peasants and from the high rate of interest on credit, thus contributing to peasants' economic unviability and consequent separation from land, and the industrialists who super-exploit urban labour and minimize demand for fresh labour from rural areas stopping peasants from getting urban work, all these industrialists are members of the same family. This means that: the fight against dispossession of peasants making room for SEZ, the fight against high prices of industrial goods used by peasants and against high interest rates, and the fight against super-exploitation of urban labour, must be all interconnected. This combined fight is the fight for a particular form of industrialization, one that would remove the differences between peasants and industry, between rural and urban areas, and that would remove the relations of exploitation between capital and labour, and would thus ensure a decent living for all working people.

From this standpoint, the current struggles around SEZs and displacement, which are important, appear to be somewhat narrow. They are often too defensive. The message of these struggles seems to be: 'don't take away our land, leave us alone (to our misery)'. The struggle against displacement should be a part of the larger family of struggles, i.e. struggles over industrialization as such. This is because the objects of struggle are objectively interconnected. The fight against SEZs must be a fight against a particular existing form of industrialization which leads to double 'dispossession': political acts of dispossession or primitive accumulation, and 'dispossession' (class differentiation) through market mechanisms (rising prices of industrial goods leading to debt and sale of assets including land). A part of the fight should also be within SEZs (and other industrialized areas). Seen in another way, the fight against SEZs and displacement is a fight for a certain form of industrialization, which, in turn, is a fight for (deepening) democracy and for the satisfaction of social, cultural and ecological needs of those who are displaced to make room for industries, those who lose land because of rising prices of industrial goods, and those who work inside the industrial areas.

## Notes

1. Protest politics against the excesses of the system does not necessarily challenge capitalist relations as such (e.g. private ownership of property; right to exploit labour; right to appropriate property of small-scale owners, etc.). But it challenges the fact that some companies make more money than other companies by using corrupt methods; payment of super-low wages (and therefore super-exploitation); dispossession of peasants without proper compensation, etc. Philosophically speaking, and in terms of a stratified ontology: a) there is a structure, b) there are the ways in which the structure operates, and c) then there are certain effects produced as a result. Protest politics is more about the last level or the last two levels.
2. Given the materiality of our body, we need food, although whether it is *roti* or *chawal* is a different matter. Given the materiality of our body, which requires protection from nature, we need safe shelter, but the actual type of house people live in may be different in different social-geographical contexts, etc.
3. I am not necessarily saying that patience in every case and all times is a virtue. When the time to launch a fundamental opposition to the social-political order comes, and if the opportunity is not used, it may not return, so it is criminal to be patient in that case. But when the majority of workers and poor peasants are not prepared to launch a fundamental opposition to power and to demand a new society where there is democracy in every sphere of life, any impatient action can be criminal as well. In this context, the reader may want to see David Laibman's (2016) *Passion and Patience*.
4. Of course, that does not mean that things cannot change quickly, almost overnight. No one had predicted that the French working class would rise in the way they did in 2016.
5. Consider how Wall Street Occupiers in New York set up public libraries, public healthcare system, public eating places, etc.
6. Of course, the pursuit of reforms must happen through proper organizational means to bear fruits.
7. That is why the Dalai Lama (2001: 91) advises the rich to be compassionate towards the poor. 'In the long run, the wealthy have nothing to gain in allowing the global situation to deteriorate. They will have to protect themselves from the resentment of the poor and will live in fear more and more, as is already the case in a number of countries. Any society where the rich are too rich and the poor too poor will generate violence, crime and civil war. Agitators can easily get the poor to rise up [against the rich]...'. India could be easily one such country that the spiritual leader is talking about.

8. The Bhoomi Adhikar Andolan (Land Rights Movement) or BAA is a new united peasant movement in India. At a convention in Gujarat in July 2016, BAA decided to support the all-India strike of workers on September 2, 2016 in which 150 million workers participated, which, Vijay Prasad says, may be the largest workers' strike in centuries.
9. This does not mean that the second kind of separation can be seen as a specific form of separation or dispossession. This sort of conflation is committed by David Harvey (2010: 311) when he says that 'The extraction of surplus-value is, after all, a specific form of accumulation by dispossession' (2010: 311). For a critique of his approach to dispossession, see Das, 2017c. We should not extinguish the theoretical difference between a) separation from property from b) exploitation in the workplace.

# 11

# The Left, and What is To Be Done About the Hindu Right?

The struggle for economic concessions, including for protection against unfair dispossession, has become a more complex issue, with the Hindu Right coming to power, when there is not only an attack on the livelihood of people but also on their democratic, including, religious, rights (see Chapters 8-9). The question posed in this Chapter is the following: now that the Right is in power, the question is what is to be done?

A wide range of thinkers, including the Buddha and modern-day radical philosophers, have said that nothing exists by itself, and that in the world there are things and then there are mechanisms underlying these things.[1] For example, if poverty exists, then conditions for poverty's existence also must exist. Poverty's conditions of existence can be many. They are objective, in the sense that they exist independently of what an individual—or even a group of individuals—thinks or does at a given point in time: these conditions include the profit-driven private property system; neoliberal policies; state's anti-democratic measures, etc.[2] Then there are subjective conditions: people struggling to remove poverty and the weaknesses in their struggle; weakness of leadership of the poor masses.

Some conditions of existence for a thing (e.g. poverty) support the thing in question, and other conditions tend to undermine it. A thing exists and continues to exist when: its conditions of existence which support it ('positive' conditions) are more powerful than the conditions of existence which undermine it ('negative' conditions).

Deployment of anti-democratic measures which stop people from launching a struggle against poverty in an effective (e.g. united) way is a 'positive' condition for the existence of poverty. People struggling to remove poverty becomes the 'negative' condition for poverty.[3]

More generally: there are various social problems, and people engage in struggles to remove them (or to significantly and sustainably alleviate their adverse consequences). Humanity has never created social problems which it cannot address.[4] Social problems are the problems that are in society and that are a barrier to people becoming what they can be in the absence of these problems. One of the ways in which social problems can be addressed is the political: i.e. political mobilization aimed at taking control of the mechanisms that are creating—that are the cause of—the social problems in question.

Now, the struggle to remove problems such as poverty must include the struggle against the positive conditions and for the negative conditions (i.e. the conditions that remove—negate—poverty).[5] This latter struggle includes the very right to struggle against the problems. To repeat: to struggle against social problems or social-ecological problems, one must struggle for the right to struggle against these problems.

The relation between the existence of a social problem and the fact that it can be removed by a struggle is not a straightforward process. It is a mediated process, a process that refers to the struggle to create conditions for the struggle against a social problem. So the struggle against problems is really a two-pronged struggle: the struggle to create conditions for the struggle and the struggle against the cause of the problems. For example, one must not only fight against the employers paying abysmally low wages, but also one must struggle for the right to launch this kind of struggle.

The struggle to create conditions for the struggle against poverty and other social problems means, among other things, the battle for democracy. In the light of the perspective offered above, the struggle for democracy must include a) the struggle for democracy where it does not exist, and b) the struggle for the continued existence of democracy where it exists, for there are always objective and subjective conditions that undermine the conditions for democracy.

Given that the bourgeoisie is increasingly 'reneging' on its promise to protect minimum democratic rights as in a liberal democracy, the struggle against poverty, etc. increasingly means—requires—a political struggle: the struggle against the attempts of the bourgeois elements to divide the nation of exploited classes (the nation of workers and poor peasants, adivasis and small-scale or those involved in collective production) along the lines of religion, region, language, and caste. The political struggle for democracy therefore includes the struggle against the conditions for the religious right and casteists to exist; the political struggle means the struggle to unite the exploited and oppressed groups so they can then struggle against the cause of the social problems, and therefore struggle against the forces which create disunity. Every political struggle is a struggle to and struggle against/over.

That is why, and to repeat: to struggle against the conditions for such things as poverty (i.e. struggle against capitalist and capitalist state policies) requires a struggle to create the conditions for that struggle: such conditions include creating ideological-political unity among the oppressed and exploited elements, and defending democratic rights to struggle. In the present Indian condition, this means that people will have to struggle for protecting democratic rights and deepening them, in the face of the attack on these rights by the state and Hindutva elements which surround the state and which are inside it. To say that some elements in the Hindutva brigade are only for development and good governance and other elements—the so-called, fringe elements—are creating the troubles on the street (e.g. lynching people for their non-Hindu religious views or practices) is an utter lie. This is the kind of lie that is based on a meticulous well-thought out political differentiation among the elements in the brigade that is being mobilized to create its opposite, i.e. a political homogenization, in the form of a homogenized Hindu nation, backed by authoritarian, Hinduized, state power and fuelled by imaginary notions of all Hindus having been hurt by non-Hindus. The purpose of some communal political homogenization is to strengthen the right-wing economic-political-cultural agenda, one that is, more or less, shared by all the elements, fringe or central. The fringe elements are exactly the kind of foot soldiers that are deployed from time to time—and especially before elections, for the brigade to come to power through elections, and whether the fringe elements or central elements. So the political struggle must be against the brigade as a totality, and not just against its specific parts, i.e. the so-called lumpen, fringe elements, who happen to be over-enthusiastic about what is otherwise a civil, polite, democratic intention of the brigade. The parts make the whole. The whole makes the parts.[6] Also, there is no doubt that large sections of the big business are in an alliance with, and support, these ultra conservative, semi-fascistic, undemocratic, elements. So the struggle for democracy will become a struggle against the political interests of the bourgeoisie directly and their economic interests indirectly, at least, initially.

What class form will such political struggle for secular democracy take? The answer is this: there is no reason why workers, small-scale self-employed producers in rural and urban areas (including poor peasants), and aboriginal peoples, and their political parties/movements, and their progressive organic intellectuals cannot come together, at multiple geographical scales, starting from a city-neighbourhood and rural hamlet (e.g. action committees or councils of workers and of peasants), with the aim of struggling for the democratic rights of these basic classes and class-fractions in the first instance. These rights include the right to practise any religion one wishes, the right to eat whatever food one chooses (beef or not), the right to be free from caste, gender, linguistic and geographical discrimination, the right to receive an education that respects scientific temper, secularism and internationalism, and not the worshipping of the so-called Hindu nation or any other sectarian version of the nation. And there is no reason why such a struggle cannot be independent of all bourgeois parties.[7] In fact, to have any traction, the political struggle must have that overall class independence vis-a-vis at least the big business parties and the big business as a class. What is needed, in India, is a class-based 'coalition' (i.e. a united front) of political forces outside the political space occupied by forces supporting the two big-business parties (Congress and BJP), in order to struggle for democracy (and for more—i.e. economic security).[8] More specifically, there is a need for a united front of workers and peasants, some of whom are communist and others who operate within circles of reformist-bourgeois ideas and practices. There is a united front in another sense: students/teachers and workers. The battle for democracy must be fought together by students who are future workers and by members of the working class (both those who are employed and who are looking for jobs): both these groups need democracy to be what they are. Students/teachers need democracy to learn/teach and debate without fear of being labelled anti-national or anti-Hindu, etc., without fear of the Hindutva type brigade insulting or hurting them. Workers need democracy to fearlessly fight employers and governments for their pro-business policies pursued in an authoritarian manner.

One may ask: on what these forces will put pressure in their political struggle? On a bourgeois government (e.g. on a Congress or BJP government in India)? Or, will these basic classes and their organic intellectuals try to form a government of their own, which will respect secularism and democracy? Or, will they remain as an extra-governmental power bloc and merely put pressure on whichever government there is, i.e. pressure for secularism, for democracy, etc., in order to create conditions for the struggle for the abolition of the bourgeois system?

These are difficult questions. But there is no doubt that: the more this political struggle consciously becomes a part of the struggle against the system of class rule as such—i.e. the more this political struggle relates the attack on democracy and people's living standards to their class origin (which therefore needs to be removed)—the more effective it will be in winning what are political-democratic demands. Major concessions are given by the ruling class when there is a threat to its class position, its position as a ruling class, to its property rights (and not merely to its political form of governance), and not necessarily solely because of the political struggle (or even the union struggle) per se.[9] There are definite limits to the extent to which in the current conjuncture a ruling class will concede to significant democratic demands. This is especially the case when the undemocratic conduct[10] has become an important way in which the ruling class in a liberal democracy rules. In India, the bourgeoisie's failure to protect people's democratic rights (including the right to freely unionize)[11] and the failure to concede to demands for meagre improvement in living standards, during the Congress regime was a condition of existence for the current attack on democracy and living standards by the Right; and the Right's attack on democracy is even more severe than in the previous regime. Congress is no paragon of democracy and secularism, but it would not attack secularism to the extent that BJP will.[12] Both parties have together shown that they—and thus the big business class whose interests they represent—are unsuitable to rule.

The Hindu Right, both within the state and outside, is the greatest threat to democracy. It must be fought on all fronts by the masses. The raw materials—conditions of existence—exist for that struggle. Thirty-one per cent per cent votes were cast for the BJP at the 2014 national election. This means that merely 20 per cent of the eligible voters, or, 14 per cent of India's population, supported it. In other words: potentially, 86 per cent of India, 80 per cent of eligible voters, and 69 per cent of the people who voted did not support the BJP. This massive force is a substantial basis for the conditions for the struggle for democracy and secularism. This is the struggle of the 69 per cent vs 31 per cent. And this 31 per cent includes many people who voted for the BJP not because they supported its obscurantist Hindutva politics and right wing pro-business policies but because Congress, BJP's other, utterly failed in meeting the needs of the people, and because there was not a credible secular alternative on offer. On the other hand, there are millions of ordinary people who vote for Left parties/ ideas/ proposals. In a large majority of Left-oriented constituencies, Left parties are major forces; they have lost only because of the faulty electoral system (the first-past-the-post system). There are millions of people in Left-oriented unions. There are progressive civil society organizations, including those of artists and writers, associated with the Left. There are secular-minded people in smaller non-Left parties (including in what are called socialist parties). India still has one of the largest concentrations of progressive intellectuals in the world who are committed to scientific and secular values, and who think from the standpoint of the working masses (workers and small-scale independent producers), however inadequately. Overall India has a large Left and secular-democratic cultural apparatus, which the saffron brigade terms pseudo-secularists and which it seeks to undermine by filling cultural institutions and institutions of higher learning with Hindutva supporters and pseudo-intellectuals, or people with doubtful intellectual calibre.[13] The Left and secular-democratic cultural apparatus needs urgent renewal and new energy, as a part of the counter-hegemonic project. With a proper class perspective which unpacks the connection between class relations and the attack on democracy and which guides a class-oriented struggle for democracy and secularism, this apparatus can potentially create conditions of the existence for the struggle against poverty and other social problems. The struggle for democratic rights (for secular democracy) is linked to the struggle for economic concessions but that struggle has its own relatively autonomous dynamics, and both the struggle for democracy and for economic concessions must be a part of, and be informed by, the struggle for a new society, one where profit for a few does not dictate production and exchange. A part of the counter-hegemonic project is to generate awareness among the masses that another world is possible, a world that is much more humane and democratic. The struggle for democracy and secularism announces to members of the bourgeoisie, whether they support rabid communalists or are formally secular, that their economic rule is in trouble, not only because it has failed to satisfy the needs of the masses while living off their labour with opulence but also because it has failed to respect the minimum standards of democracy. As long as the moneybags (the top 1 per cent or so), can make lots of money, they do not care if democratic rights, including the rights of religious minorities, are respected or not.

## Conclusion

The BJP government on assuming to power in 2014 recommended the promulgation of ordinances for auction of coal blocks and increasing the foreign investment ceiling for insurance from 26 per cent to 49 per cent. Given the determined resistance to its reforms agenda from the opposition, it failed to get the bills passed in parliament. Replying to a question as to what was the urgency to bring an ordinance a day after the winter session concluded, the Finance Minister said: 'There has been too much delay. That is why there is urgency.' The Minister was concealing the real cause for urgency. But he could not entirely hide his feelings for the economic masters. He said: 'It [the ordinance] announces to the rest of the world, including investors, that this country can no longer wait even if one of the Houses of Parliament waits indefinitely to take up its agenda' (*Hindu* 2014). So, democratic method or not, the government is keen on paying back the bourgeoisie which placed it in power through its money power (the recent attempt to privatize forests and turn them over to the big business is just one example). The government will not wait. If the government exercises this kind of urgency in trying to appease its masters (the bourgeoisie) and can discard the democratic pretence, the masses must show a similar kind of urgency and announce to the political class and its economic class masters their own intention: to take control over their own political destiny, that they also cannot wait eternally.

In society as in nature, there are different levels at which things exist: things, and then conditions of existence of things. Society comprises economic, political and cultural facets/

aspects. To the extent that this is true, progressives, i.e. those who speak on behalf of workers and small-scale producers, must struggle for a popular democratic consciousness, a democratic culture, democratic political rights and secularism, all of which will constitute conditions for the struggle against an economic system which is based on money and profits rather than on the direct satisfaction of human needs in a manner that is collective in nature and that is sustainable both socially and ecologically. A struggle for democracy becomes a condition of existence for, and is not at all unrelated to, the struggle for a collective control over society's resources.

When the bourgeois society is in crisis, it resorts to irrationalism—un-reason—of all sorts. This happens not just in India. Consider the former British Prime Minister characterizing Britain as a Christian country. Whether in India or Britain or elsewhere, it is increasingly clear that the ruling class has scant regard for the values which it had earlier relied on in order to produce consent to its rule: these values include not only democracy but also secularism.[14] The critique of a society must start with a critique of the social conditions giving rise to religious views and practices which have an adverse impact on public life, and specifically of the ways in which religion is made use of to reproduce and reinforce a deeply in-egalitarian social order.

The broader social-political movement of the Hindu Right and the Gujarat model (or Modani model) of development as its specific vehicle (a labouratory) and purpose are simply unacceptable in every way that one can rationally imagine. It must be subjected to complete rejection, which must be a part of the rejection of the wider model of which it is a part. And the Right model should be rejected, and inside and outside the national and state-level legislatures, and in every possible fora, in teashops, and coffee houses, in universities and colleges, and on the streets. The Hindu Right is the single most important immediate threat to the country's collective democratic conscience, including the right to dissent on the part of ordinary citizens, writers, artists, students, professors, media people, and progressives in different sectors of society. To relish and value the lofty and humanistic ideas in Hinduism and in other religions where they exist and feel proud of the existence of these ideas,[15] one does not need interventions of communalists, nor does one need to hate one religion to be able to value another religion. The Hindutva politics and Hindutva way of thinking constitutes the most dangerous affront to the rich democratic, secular tradition of India, and to the legitimate aspirations of toiling men, women and children of all religions, castes and provinces, to lead a comfortable life. The battle for democracy must be connected to the fight for economic concessions, and both forms of the fight must be fought within a larger framework, one that prioritizes common people's need over the private profit for a few. Ultimately, the only way to fight to root out communalization of society and polity and to ensure that ordinary people have a life of economic security is to mobilize them on the basis of an agenda that puts the collective control of society's resources and polity in their own hands. And for that to happen, a massive change in consciousness is required.

## Notes

1. The above follows from an ontology of stratification in the tradition of critical realism of Roy Bhaskar, Andrew Sayer, etc. and from the tradition of materialist dialectics itself. These traditions say that the world is a layered entity; the reality exists at multiple levels. This idea is opposed to the flat ontology idea, that is used by most people, experts or laypeople.
2. See Sayer (2000) for multiple meanings of 'objective'.
3. 'Positive' and 'negative' are not used here in the sense of what is good or what is bad.
4. I am paraphrasing this statement from Marx: 'Mankind thus inevitably sets itself only such tasks as it is able to solve, since closer examination will always show that the problem itself arises only when the material conditions for its solution are already present or at least in the course of formation'. Available at: https://www.marxists.org/archive/marx/works/1859/critique-pol-economy/preface.htm
5. It also follows that if poverty is a consequence of another deeper-level mechanism (i.e. class), then, the struggle against poverty must be, ultimately, a struggle against class.

6. The case of the saffron brigade spreading communal poison raises an interesting philosophical question. Godse, associated with the RSS, killed Gandhi yet the RSS would like people to think that the RSS could not be accused of killing someone who is widely considered the father of the nation. When Muslims are killed by the Hindus in communal riots, it is claimed that the individuals who are fringe elements do this, and that the individuals who work as the political and ideological leaders at various levels have nothing to do with it. However, it is clear that the saffron structure (consisting of various civil society associations, small and large political parties, vigilante groups, ideological organizations, think-tanks, etc.) would not exist without the daily interventions of specific individuals within that structure. What exactly is the relation between the structure and the individuals? Are the individuals really as dispensable as the managers of the saffron structure claim? Or, is it that some individuals can be claimed as legitimate, and others not? No structure can be reproduced without the actions of individuals, no matter how unconscious or semi-conscious they may be about the objective effects of what they do. Perhaps an ideological mechanism through which the saffron structure is reproduced and gains its acceptance is by creating a multi-tier structure, one in which there are so-called fringe individuals and non-fringe individuals, the difference and connection between whom can be adjusted as the political conjuncture demands.
7. However, only on tactical grounds, and conjuncturally, may such a movement be supported by parties/movements of regional/small-scale bourgeois property owners and urban educated upper middle class as long as they show a consistent commitment to secular democracy and to public policies aimed at a significant improvement in the lives of the masses.
8. See Choonera (2007), Riddel (2011) and Trotsky (1922; 1931), on the united front.
9. As is widely known now, democratic measures and welfare benefits have been granted in the West and elsewhere more or less because of the threat of a 1917 (or 1949 perhaps) there.
10. An attack on secularism is an attack on democracy: it is an attack on the idea that all persons, irrespective of their religious beliefs, are equal before the law.
11. As Prabhat Patnaik notes recently, the main aim of labour reforms is really not to give the power to employers to hire and fire, that power they have over 96 per cent of the workers already; the main aim is to be able to stop workers from unionizing.
12. There are individuals within Congress (e.g. Kapil Sibal) who are committed to secular democracy in their public life.
13. The Right in India as a coherent political movement is relatively new and it simply has a limited sophisticated theoretical perspective on major

problems/issues such as agrarian change, democracy, state, economic development, etc., which a) is its own (i.e. which has grown out of the political and social experience of the participants of the movement), b-c) can defend itself against theoretical critique from alternative approaches, and be backed by evidence, and d) enjoys the prestige/recognition of the alternative approaches to society and life that exist in society. This is why the Right often uses muscle power and uncivil behaviour in order to make people accept its intellectually inadequate and socially regressive views.

14. Secularism in the sense of the separation of the state/politics from religion which should be a matter concerning people's private lives (and people should have the freedom to practise any religion they wish or not to practise any religion at all). Public resources must not be spent on any religious purpose, even in the name of the state giving equal protection to all religions. Socialism of state support for religions is no secularism.
15. Once again, people must have the freedom to practise any religion and as a part of their practice, they can value the good aspects of a religion while maintaining a critical attitude towards it at all times. One's own view about their preferred religion cannot be allowed to be a cause of harm to the followers of another religion.

# 12

# The Left, and the Political Consciousness of the Masses

The Left has suffered one electoral defeat after another, especially since the 2009 and 2014 national elections in India. Its electoral strength at the national level (in terms of the number of Members of Parliament who are directly elected) has been considerably reduced. How the current economic crisis plays itself out, and with what implications for workers and peasants in India, will in good part depend on how the crisis of the Indian Left is resolved. A few preliminary thoughts are offered here about this defeat.

The electoral defeat of the Indian Left (e.g. the CPI-M and CPI) is unfortunate, if not unexpected. But history has provided the Left with an opportunity for rethinking its political strategy. It is true that the success or failure of Left forces cannot and should not be judged (solely or even mainly) by its electoral performance. If the electoral loss was the only form of loss, it would not be a cause for much concern. But the electoral loss experienced by the Left is also indicative of the fact that most segments of the Left which participate in elections have not spent as much energy as they should on radical mass movements of the marginalized, and especially rural and urban workers, poor peasants and petty entrepreneurs/traders, at local, regional and national scales. The Left forces who fight in elections spend most of their limited political energy on elections per se or matters directly related to elections. To the extent that it is important for them to fight in elections, electoral fights must be rooted in, and grow out of, their participation in, and leadership of, class-based (democratically-organized) movements. Elections must be used for ideological and mobilizational purposes—for educating the masses and sections of the (urban) middle class about the failure of the ruling classes and their governments and about the potential for radical change, and not primarily to occupy positions within the state.

## Contradictions of the Left

The Left's contradictions emanate from, and reflect, the fact that the Left's ideology and practice are one thing at the centre of the Indian state in Delhi and another in the states. There are two points to be made here.

Firstly, the dominant focus on elections at the expense of extra-electoral struggle, along with the strategy of supporting one bourgeois political formation after another (Janata coalition, Congress coalition, etc.) at the national level have meant that: these formations, and especially Congress, the traditional party of the bourgeoisie and landlords, have been able to implement blatantly right-wing neoliberal policies. The fact that Mr. Manmohan Singh, a former economics professor who belongs to the Congress and a former Prime Minister, and others constantly refer to reforms with a human face mean that the so-called reforms are essentially inhuman and must be seen as such. On the other hand, to the extent that the Left puts pressure on the national government to implement a few poor-poor policies such as the employment guarantee scheme in rural areas, it is the parties running the government and especially the Congress that take the credit for these policies. As a result, these parties get votes from the poor in exchange for a few crumbs reluctantly thrown at them. So, the Left does not get credit for the good thing it does (i.e. pro-poor policies it forces the national government to implement; some kind of government regulation over the financial sector which has allowed the nation to avert the worst consequences of the economic crisis so far).

The Left is also discredited in another sense. Thanks to the hegemony of neoliberal ideology, development is construed as market-led development. Given that development is the mantra for winning elections, and to the extent that the Left has slowed down some market-reforms at the national level, it is portrayed by the bourgeois media and politicians and by the bourgeoisie itself as an obstacle to development as such. Who does not want 'development', and who wants a political formation which is not for 'development'? 'Development'—often packaged as bijli, sadak, pani (electricity, roads and water) in the vast rural periphery and elsewhere has become a big bourgeois ideology. This is an ideology which helps the ruling classes and their political representatives to buy consent from people.

Secondly, in the subnational states where the Left is in power, it behaves like a version of 'Left Congress' at best. This it cannot do. It just cannot criticize the same policies of the central government which it itself adopts in the states in which it rules. By shaking hands with big-business, domestic or foreign, and implementing some of the neoliberal policies, the Left allows bourgeois parties (in their regional incarnations and often in their demagogic forms) to opportunistically bear the mantle of pro-poor parties in Left-ruled states and to gain electoral advantage. This is exactly what happened in the largest Left bastion (West Bengal). The Left, of course, does this in the name of creating jobs (as one Left leader put it to me: unless there are industries, there is no working class to mobilize). But dispossessing peasants of their land against their wish cannot be the Left method of creating industrial employment. The fact that the Left followed this method signifies how far to the Right the Left has moved.

Jobs can be created; people's productive power can be developed; modern technology can be adopted (and if necessary obtained from foreign sources); and people can expand their needs which make for a better quality of life. All these and many other things can happen under a variety of social relations of ownership and control of property. A factory owned by the (big) bourgeoisie (on land from which poor peasants have been forcefully displaced) indicates one type of relations. A democratically-run cooperative of (women) workers (producing, in an ecologically sound manner, a thing that satisfies a need of a vast majority of the local/national population) indicates another. Where and when in power, the Left really must show that jobs can be created under a different framework of social relations than those that are corporate-dominated. It is the corporate domination of our lives that both the ruling-class parties (i.e. Congress and BJP) support in exactly equal measure. This, unfortunately, most ordinary people do not understand, and changing this situation is a major ideological challenge for the Left.

Whether the Left should run state governments and for what purpose and how is a matter of debate. To the extent that Left-governed states will exist, jobs must be created in a manner in which it is consistent with the Left's ideological premises (one of which is the democratic control over the means of production to be used for the satisfaction of basic material-cultural needs of people). Otherwise, the connection between Left theory and Left praxis is broken. It has been broken in the Left states, which is why many people—including parts of the middle class—may not find much difference in economic policy between the Left and the two mainstream parties (both of which may chant some anti-poverty rhetoric and/or even throw some crumbs at the poor to buy their votes) and especially between the Left and Congress.

## Mass Movements and Mass Education

Let me return to the issue of 'mass' movements. One important reason for organizing these movements is to demand immediate relief for the oppressed and exploited from factory owners, (upper caste) landlords and capitalist farmers, big traders and governments. But perhaps more importantly, these movements shape class consciousness of the poor and enhance their political power, which may, from time to time, bear electoral results (which is secondary). In turn, both elections and mass movements—both kinds of Left practice—presuppose ideological education of the masses. The cause becomes the effect and the effect becomes the cause. Local reading groups and working-class based cultural associations, among other things, are important here. The political energy of the oppressed and exploited workers can and must be channelled in productive and progressive directions, the energy that the mainstream parties electorally mobilize in order to continue the current system where a few are growing richer while the vast majority are eking out a minimal existence. The Left must be a part of the everyday life of workers and peasants.

Here it is important to stress the role of the 'middle class' in relation to the revival of the Left. The 'middle class' includes not only the better-paid and educated parts of the working class but also independent educated small entrepreneurs, many of whom happen to be private proprietors because decent salaried work is not available. The urban middle class of the air-conditioned mall must feel that it is 'cool' to be on the Left. They must feel that it is 'un-cool' to accept (American) imperialism, communalism and the principle of corporate greed. They must feel that it is 'un-cool' to accept a system where the country's land, forests, water, minerals, plantations, and machines are owned and controlled by just a minority of the population who determine how well we live and how, where we live, etc. Vast segments of this middle class must understand that the inequality between the rich and the poor (and more specifically the control of our major resources in the hands of a few, and associated exploitation) is not un connected to such factors as caste and gender oppression as well as ecological destruction and corruption in private and public sectors, the things which many conscientious middle class people find easy to relate to. The urban middle class must find it 'cool' that the Left agenda is to form a society where there is plenty of leisure, where there are parks, sports facilities, modern public transit, theatres, etc. available for free or at highly subsidized rates, where there are coops managed by women selling organic food, artisanal goods, and similar items, where there is modern subsidized housing, and where there are publicly provided high-quality education and decent and secure work for everyone.

One must have faith in 'ideological development and transformation': when we work on our ideas, our ideas about the world change. Running reading groups and discussing radical theory as well as current Left policies/actions (including their shortcomings which are inevitable) in a polite and democratic manner can contribute to a change in the consciousness of sections of the middle class. A large number of middle class people may just care about themselves. But not everyone of them falls in this category. There are many who seriously think that they can make a difference to the world of the poor through individual charity, through participation in political parties of the rich and through some NGO activities. The challenge for the Left is to patiently show that while these things are not absolutely useless modes of intervening in the world, they have severe limitations because they do not challenge the sources of power of the rich in their control over property and indeed over knowledge (think about newspapers and TV channels owned for profit by big business). They must also understand that not only are BJP and Congress not alternatives, the Aam Admi Party (AAP) is also not an alternative.[1]

I can say this on the basis of my own experience as a university teacher: when middle class people who join the university as students are helped—both in the classroom and outside—to understand the logic of a theory of society which seeks to grasp everything by its roots and which seeks to scientifically explain various forms of oppression and exploitation with a passionate motive to eradicate these, other competing systems of thought which they have been imbued with all their lives start not making sense to them any more. The more they learn new ideas, the more they unlearn old ideas. Demystification of the reality slowly begins to happen. The present system can continue as long as the vast majority believe that what is happening is natural, that it is natural that some people will despotically control our productive resources under whom the rest have to work for a wage/salary. An important aim of ideological education is to denaturalize the current state of affairs. One of the biggest losses of the Left is the loss of emphasis on political-ideological education of ordinary workers and peasants as well as sections of the urban middle class. What the Left has lost is the sympathy of a segment of the middle class. This must be reversed through patient ideological activity in a democratic manner (one in which radical teachers, among others, have an important role to play). Ideas of the Left must be a part of the common sense of a very large section of the population, including segments of the middle class as well as the working class and poor peasants. After all, the majority need to be convinced that an anti-capitalist ideology and a vision of a society which is not dominated by the profit-motive, make sense.

It cannot be forgotten at all that whenever there is a possibility of Left resurgence, main bourgeois-political forces (e.g. Congress and BJP) will be, covertly/overtly, united, and the ruling classes will not have any problem with it at all. It may be noted that less than 50 per cent of voters endorse either BJP or Congress, the two mainstream parties, which means that even from an electoral standpoint, there is a massive space within which to expand the Left electoral appeal if this appeal is constructed in terms of the firm support for the interests of workers and peasants, oppressed lower castes and women, deprived regions and for a secular polity. The political forces of the Left must be mobilized independently of, and in opposition to, both these bourgeois-landlord parties. The future of the majority of India's population depends on the political and ideological strength of Left and democratic forces in every nook and corner of the country.

India has a large number of Left parties, many of them with long traditions of struggle against injustice. They include not only the two major communist parties (CPI and CPI-M) but also smaller parties which are traditionally a part of a Left front government. There are then Left parties of the Naxalite variety, who follow Maoism. Of these parties, CPI-Maoist is only one. CPI Liberation, which is involved in joint struggles with CPI and CPI-M, and many other Naxalite parties operate in different areas. Then there are many smaller revolutionary-Marxist groups. They define the current stage of revolution not as merely democratic. They, quite rightly, believe that democratic revolution must be a part of an uninterrupted transition to a socialist struggle: struggle for democratic revolution must be a part of the struggle for socialism (Das, 2017a). There is no reason why class conscious workers and poor peasants as well as students/teachers of many of these Left parties/movements cannot come together in a united front on one or another issue at a given point of time (e.g. to fight communalism; ecological damage; dispossession of small-scale producers; attack on the right to unionize; decline in spending on welfare; tax concessions and de facto loan waivers for the rich business houses; India's policies making it subservient to imperialism in the military sphere, etc.). In the process, and gradually, a foundation can be laid for a broader Left unity which would militantly fight for democratic rights and economic concessions, consciously making that fight a part of the fight for a society which is not guided by the profit motive and dominated by private property relations.

## The Coming Challenge

Every defeat is a challenge. That is the law of dialectics in real life. Without Left support to hold parliamentary power, the national Congress-led government that existed before 2014 would have certainly implemented even more blatantly pro-business policies. In fact, without the Left presence, including the trade union movement, most governments would be more rightwing than they have been.[2] The new BJP government, like its predecessor Congress government did, will use the pretext of the current economic crisis to implement policies that benefit big business at the expense of workers and peasants in the name of helping the latter. Big business and its media have already prodded the government to implement these policies. The implementation of these pro-business policies, in a situation of growing unemployment, has contributed to the economic crisis in India, a crisis of livelihood, and, of development. The policies are bound to sharpen the class conflict between the bourgeoisie and its government on the one hand and workers and peasants on the other. With the Left forces not obliged to support an existing government, this is a great opportunity for them to do what they should have been doing all along: mobilize workers and peasants to fight for democratic rights and for the rights of religious minorities, of women and lower castes and adivasis, and for major economic concessions (including a living wage, secure jobs, and free or highly-subsidized healthcare and education, etc. as well as remunerative prices for independent farmers) as a part of the fight against the system of private property and production based on profit. Even if the Left has to support a slightly progressive government to keep the fascistic forces at bay and stop them from using state power to further their regressive agenda, the Left should do this, as long as its main focus remains on extra-electoral mobilization of the masses; indeed removing the right-wing forces from power will remove a major obstacle to the extra-electoral mobilization of the masses. The Left should mobilize its ideological and political forces in the states where it is traditionally strong (West Bengal, Tripura and Kerala) against communalism and neoliberalism in the interest of defending the democratic and social rights of the masses. In the constituencies where the Left is relatively weak, it may enter into a tactical understanding with non-fascistic bourgeois political parties in order to maximize the electoral support for secular forces and minimize the division of anti-BJP votes, on the condition that the secular political parties will implement progressive economic policies. The fight to defend the democratic rights, including the rights of religious minorities, must be linked to the fight against the attack on the living standards of the workers and small-scale producers. These two fights, when they happen together, will increase the strength of each fight. Any government that is non-communal but that implements right-wing economic policies in the interest of the business class will just create conditions for the return of communal forces.

## Notes

1. AAP is simply a bourgeois party. The AAP people are—and are for—true capitalists. The Party is for capitalism, but it is for a specific form of capitalism, one that is corruption-free. It is a capitalism where there is a level playing field for all capitalists, none among whom benefits from undue connections to the government. Consider what AAP says on its website: 'AAP deeply believes that entrepreneurship and industry [read: capitalism] are the life blood of the economy. What we are against is companies indulging in corruption - paying political parties to seek favours, bribing their way to contracts, etc. ...[M]any of our established industrial houses are products of the license raj. They have grown and thrived by nurturing corruption. They are uncomfortable with true free enterprise where transparency and competition are the basis for all contracts and ongoing renewal of business. ...So please remember that AAP is not against industry. We are committed to industrial growth and entrepreneurship provided it is corruption free. We wish to break the nexus between business and political parties and establish a level playing field that will unleash a host of opportunities for entrepreneurs across the country.'

   AAP is typical of that political tendency which is deeply ideological by rejecting the idea of being ideological. The party is not only ideological but deeply opportunistic; it is proud to be able to turn left and right when the situation demands. The party says:

   'There is an age-old tendency to pin down political parties as left, right, centre, etc. In the process everyone forgets the issues at hand and their solutions. Our goal is to remain solution focused. If the solution to a problem lies on the left we are happy to consider it. Likewise if it is on the right (or in the centre) we are equally happy to consider it. Ideology is one for the pandits and the media to pontificate about. We are solution focused rather than ideology driven.'

   Like many other similar reformist bourgeois and petty bourgeois formations, AAP is under the illusion that people can successfully fight to democratize the system and produce a more honest and accountable administration without fighting against the class logic, the logic of profit making which underlies most gross forms of unaccountability and corruption. Corruption is not just in the government. It is in the private sector. Business people, in order to increase their competitiveness, bribe this or that government official or politician. The origin of corruption is very much in the private sector. And Aam Aadmi is for the private sector and it is against crony capitalism, it is against the more politically connected business players. The fact that AAP believes that curtailing inflation or making available water or electricity at lower rates is possible raises the wider issue of political economy, issues surrounding who controls society's resources and how they are being used (people's needs or profit).

# 13

# Significance of a Counter-Hegemonic Left Culture

Capitalism creates poverty in various ways including by exploiting and over-exploiting workers, by making workers redundant through profit-seeking technical changes, and by dispossessing small-scale producers. Given that capitalism is an exploitative system, it prompts the masses to struggle against it, so capitalism requires poverty partly because poverty acts as a disciplining force on the masses. Capitalism causes and requires massive social and geographical inequality. And capitalism is inherently crisis-prone: capitalists collectively produce goods and services but cannot sell them all, so they cannot retrieve the money invested, which is when the system comes to a standstill. Workers remain un- and under-employed. Productive powers remain un- and under-used. We have just witnessed a major global economic crisis in 2008. In part because of its crisis-proneness, modern world capitalism is necessarily imperialist: advanced capitalist countries try to shift the effects of the crises they experience to politically and economically weaker countries (often with the connivance of the state in these countries). Normal mechanisms of capitalism and the combination of economic crisis and imperialism have major adverse impacts on the living conditions of the working masses in general and workers and poor peasants in the less developed countries such as India in particular.

No system of injustice goes unchallenged, however. Away from the preoccupations of the corporate-controlled mainstream

The fact that the electoral success of th
seen as an alternative must be partly seen
the Left, failure in ideological, political and
Left has failed to organize the masses on the
Indeed, sheer accommodation to the capitalist
entire Left. It merely seeks to make the system a
a little corruption free, a little more tolerable. It is
political climate in which formations like AAP em

2. This does not necessarily justify the support of the government. An important question to ask is: whil bay, what was done to raise class consciousness of th mobilize them independently of bourgeois formations outside Parliament?

media, people's movements against the profit-driven system have been taking place. Consider, for example, the Arab Spring, various social justice movements in India and elsewhere, as well as the 'occupy movements' in the US and Europe, which are bound to leave an impression on the radical imagination of the masses, even if they are being repressed. Consider the fact that there have been 17 general strikes in India between the advent of neoliberal capitalism in 1991 and now (2016). Humans have an irrepressible quest for justice and have a desire for a humane world. These various movements have emerged in response to the heightened levels of exploitation of workers, massive amount of dispossession of peasants from their property, undemocratic control over socio-economic activity and the government by large companies, and the irreparable ecological devastation and cultural impoverishment.

Many activists and movements have been inspired in their thinking by Marx's critique and other progressive scholars of capitalist commodification and development. Ideologically, these protests and the recent economic crises call into question the legitimacy not only of capitalism, including its neoliberal form, but also of capitalist nation-states and global 'state' apparatuses (e.g. World Bank and IMF). This happens in richer countries and in poorer countries such as India as well.

There has indeed been an extraordinary resurgence of interest in a Marxist worldview recently, which as Eagleton (2011) expressed it, is the most theoretically rich and politically uncompromising critique of the capitalist system. The process of resurgence of this intellectually insurgent worldview has been helped by the fact that the social relations of authoritarian 'communism', and other related views, which had acted as a fetter on the development of productive powers of Marxist research, have been burst asunder. In this context, the question of alternatives to capitalism (beyond Keynesianism, state-bureaucratism, and neo-populism)—and the role of (Marxist) intellectuals whether in academy, in the media or 'civil society' in radical social change—are being actively discussed the world over. This has led to a series of important interventions rethinking political parties, democracy and visions of viable socialisms. More and more people are reading Marx and Marxists, and reading them critically, for Marxism is a science which must be updated where necessary and which must be constantly self-critical. There is an outpouring of Marxist discussions in journals such as New York-based *Science and Society*, world's longest continuously published Marxist journal, which celebrated its 75th anniversary in October 2011, *Review of Radical Political Economics* (from Cornell University), *Historical Materialism* (from SOAS, London), *Capital and Class*, etc. Much of this resurgence is exhibited online, *Radical Notes* being a testimony to this as is, for example, *Sanhati* in India.

The remaking of socialist visions—which emphasize socialism as the flourishing of the optimal level of democracy in all spheres of human life—has also meant extensive considerations of race, caste, tribality, gender, sexuality and disability. These issues of social oppression/discrimination are important in their own right. But they are important dominantly because of the ways in which capitalism subordinates them to its own logic. Capitalism furthers its accumulation projects by using these sources of oppression to define certain working subjects as less than average workers who can be paid lower compensations. Capital also politically dominates the suffering subjects (workers and small-scale producers, including peasants) by dividing them on the basis of these non-class identities. An aspect of the resurgence of Marxist research is the immense popularity of Marxist dialectics as a holistic way of looking at the capitalist world, in terms of its unity as well as difference, from the standpoint of radically changing it. Such a dialectical method allows us to reflect on various methods of exploitation and social oppression as interconnected and as forming a concrete whole.

Reading Marx and those who engage in what the American Marxist, Hal Draper called 'Marx's Marxism' would be more than apt at a political moment when neoliberalism, in theory and practice, is in crisis, when the turbulence of capitalist economies is part of daily life. As the geographer, David Harvey and others have rightly argued, Marx is, in many ways, more relevant now than he was during his own time.

> [T]his historical moment, the one we are living in now, is the best not the worst, the most not the least appropriate moment to bring back Marx... Marx is more relevant than ever, because he, more effectively than any other human being then or now, devoted his life to explaining the systemic logic of capitalism. (Wood, 1997)

The problems caused by capitalism, and globalizing capitalism, are everywhere. These problems are, however, particularly acute in less developed countries and in the most under-developed parts of these poor countries. In many under-developed regions of India (e.g. Bihar and Odisha), capitalist market relations in land and labour coexist with remnants of coercive production relations in some localities and with highly undemocratic relations of casteism, patriarchy and tribalism more generally. The institutions of the state are more or less direct 'instruments' of property-owners, including those whose main object is to subject natural resources and working people to cruel forms of commodification and ruthless forms of exploitation, all in the name of development and dollars (export earnings). There is an inverse relation between democratic rhetoric and its actual content. There is an absence of democratic values both in the economy or polity: ordinary people have no real democratic control over the way our resources and abilities to work are used. The cult of violence is everywhere. There is systemic violence as the violence caused when people's livelihood is snatched from them or when people do not have the money to buy basic necessities because of which they starve to death or suffer from poverty-caused diseases. Related to this violence is the violence committed by specific individuals: in some places ordinary people, often out of sheer desperation, tend to resort to violence (which is unproductive in the long run), in response to which and often to preempt which the state resorts to massive and disproportionate violence.

The situation in more under-developed regions of India and in similar other countries raises several questions. Why are these regions so poor when they are so rich in terms of natural resources and labouring quality of their workers and peasants? How does capitalism make use of undemocratic social and economic relations? What explains the inability of the political and intellectual elite to help the suffering masses in any significant way? Why is it that the majority of Indians have no access to nutritious food, decent housing and clothing, quality education and healthcare as well as other amenities including safe drinking water and electricity? These and many other questions can be fruitfully explored only if we have an adequate understanding of capitalism as such and the ways in which it works in concrete circumstances. Understanding Marx is therefore essential. A proper understanding of Marx and his legacy would also make it clear to people that the Marxist vision is a vision of a society which is authentically democratic and that Marxism has little to do with any political activity which is aimed at hurting individuals in a sectarian and anarchistic style. Individuals are bearers of social relations. What needs to be changed is the system of social relations, not (just) occupiers of positions in the system.

To understand the world, it is not enough to have sense-data. We need theory, in part because important aspects of the world are not immediately accessible to mere empirical observation. There is a need to make sense of things happening not in our immediate surroundings but in society as a whole. We need to understand the interconnections among things in different spheres of life (the cultural, economic, political, ecological, etc.) and interconnections of things that are geographically located in different parts of a country and the world (e.g. working class unions or factory production in one country are connected to those in other countries). To understand the world from the standpoint of the majority, the working masses, we need a theory 'from their standpoint'. Radical transformation in the direction of social, economic and ecological democracy and justice is not possible without a radical theory. Marx and his legacy provide such a theory.

It is necessary to set up radical/progressive reading groups in different places in India (and other countries) to promote a counter-hegemonic culture, a tradition of radical imagination in theory. Consisting of interested academics, activists, workers-peasants, and indeed anyone who is interested in critically understanding the current situation with a view to radically transcending it and deepening the democratic content/spirit of our society to the highest extent possible, this group could meet regularly to read Marxist literature and non-Marxist progressive literature (e.g. indigenous socialist literature; literature from the very important Ambedkarite tradition, etc.) on topics of classical and contemporary significance and discuss it in a comradely and non-sectarian manner. It will also connect the readings and the discussions to the world around us and draw theoretical implications for political practice. There are thousands of progressive people engaged in the theoretical-political struggle for justice. Often in terms of theory, politics and method of struggles, there are 'deep' divisions among them (including, and interestingly, over the fact of whether poor countries such as India are dominantly capitalist or not). Perhaps an understanding of Marx and his legacy would show that the divisions, in some areas, are not as real as they appear to be, and that there is cause more for unity and less for division: at least the divisions should be discussed in the light of theoretical discussions the foundation for which was laid by Marx, and by Lenin in the 20$^{th}$ century. These reading groups cannot only read radical academic literature but also encourage performance of radical art in its various forms and reflect on these theoretically. The reading groups can discuss why and how it is important to fight for democratic rights and for economic concessions but also why and how such a fight is limited unless it also becomes a part of a broader fight, the fight for a new society where resources are used in the collective interests and not for individual profit. Reading groups can critically reflect on the nature of the new society where politicians will be of, and for, workers, small-scale producers and students (future workers), and where intellectuals/teachers are immersed in the culture of workers and peasants.

A culture that accurately reflects the interest and ideas of the majority of the people is a most democratic process to promote. Setting up Marxist readings groups in different parts of India (and in other countries in South Asia and elsewhere) is therefore an important need of the hour. These groups will aim to promote not only a democratic consciousness but also a consciousness of the necessity and possibility of a society where society's resources, including natural resources, are owned and controlled by all those who do the work and are used to directly satisfy people's material and cultural needs, and not to satisfy the appetite for profit (i.e. wealth in the abstract form) of a tiny minority. The fact that the richest 1 per cent of Indians own more than half of the country's wealth and that 90 per cent of Indians own less than a quarter of the country's wealth, that there is an increasing attack on people's democratic rights and on secular principles, and that the country's politics and interests are being surrendered to imperialist powers in the most anti-national manner (and this is done by politicians of all hues, including by those who swear by nationalism), means that there is a strong need to develop a culture of struggle against all these. Such a struggle has to be in the realm of consciousness as well as outside, and must promote a spirit of civil but ruthless criticism of everything that exists.

# References/Bibliography


Alavi, H. 1972. The State in Post-Colonial Societies: Pakistan and Bangladesh. *New Left Review* 74, No. 1.

Amin-Khan, T. 2012. *The Post-Colonial State in the Era of Capitalist Globalization: Historical, Political and Theoretical Approaches to State Formation*. New York: Routledge.

ASSOCHAM, 2013. Bandh Proves More Damaging to the Economy http://assocham.org/newsdetail.php?id=3908.

Banerjee, S. 1984. *India's Simmering Revolution: The Naxalite Uprising*. London: Zed.

Bera, S. 2018. Farm Suicides in 2016 Lowest in Two Decades, https://www.livemint.com/Politics/aLxCMG7keV44dNzSt4J8XK/Farm-suicides-in-2016-lowest-in-two-decades.html.

Bhagwati, J. and Panagariya, A. 2013. *India's Tryst with Destiny: Debunking the Myths that Undermine Progress and Addressing New Challenges*. Noida: HarperCollins.

Bhalla, G. 2007. *Indian Agriculture Since Independence*. Delhi: National Book Trust.

Banerjee-Guha, S. 2009. 'Neoliberalising the 'Urban': New Geographies of Power and Injustice in Indian Cities.' *Economic and Political Weekly* XLIV, No. 22.

Banaji, J., ed. 2013. *Fascism: Essays on Europe and India*. Gurgaon: Three Essays Collective.

Bardhan, P. 1998. *The Political Economy of Development in India*. Oxford: Blackwell.

Bhagwati, J. 2001. 'Growth, Poverty and Reforms.' *Economic and Political Weekly* 36, No. 10: 843-846.

Chakravarty, M. 2015. Richest 1% Own 53% of India's Wealth. *Live Mint*, https://www.livemint.com/Money/VL5yuBxydKzZHMetfC97HL/Richest-1-own-53-of-Indias-wealth.html.

Chandrasekhar, C.P. and Ghosh, J. 2012. Of Profits and Growth. Macroscan. http://www.macroscan.org/fet/may12/fet290512Profits_Growth.htm.

____. 2013. The Looming Banking Crisis. *The Hindu Businessline*. http://www.thehindubusinessline.com/opinion/columns/c-p-chandrasekhar/the-looming-banking-crisis/article5086242.ece

____. 2014. Have Workers in Gujarat Benefited from "Development"? *The Hindu Businessline*. http://www.thehindubusinessline.com/opinion/columns/c-p-chandrasekhar/have-workers- in-gujarat-benefited-from-development/article5855349.ece.

Chandrasekhar, C.P. 2012. Roaring 2000s, http://www.thehindu.com/opinion/columns/Chandrasekhar/the-roaring2000s/Chapter3403450.ece.

Chattopadhyay, K. 2014. India, Sangh Parivar and BJP: Communal Fascism and its Dangers. *Europe Solidaire Sans Frontières*. http://www.europe-solidaire.org/spip.php?article33310.

Choonera, J. 2007. The United Front. *International Socialism*, No. 117. http://isj.org.uk/the-united-front/.

Dalai Lama. 2001. Daily Advice from the Heart. Gurgaon: Harper Collins.

Das, D. and Basu, D. 2013. What Ails the Indian Economy? *Sanhati*. http://sanhati.com/excerpted/8167/.

Das, R. 1999. The Spatiality of Class and State Power: The Case of Indian Land Reforms. *Environment and Planning* A 31, No. 12: 2103-2126.

____. 2000. The State-Society Relation: The Case of an Anti-poverty Policy. *Environment and Planning C: Government and Policy* 18, No. 6: 631-650.

____. 2001a. The Political Economy of India. *New Political Economy* 6, No. 1: 103-117.

____. 2001b. Class, Capitalism and Agrarian Transition: A Review and Critique of Some Recent Arguments. *Journal of Peasant Studies* 29, No. 1: 155-174.

____. 2006. Marxist Theories of the State. In *Alternative Theories of the State*, ed. S. Pressman. New York: Palgrave Macmillan.

____. 2009. 'Looking, But Not Seeing: The State and/as Class in Rural India.' *Journal of Peasant Studies* 34, No. 3: 408-440.

____. 2010. Communalism, Business Houses, Citizenship and Gujurate. *Socialist Project Review*. http://www.socialistproject.ca

____. 2011. Significance of a Counter-Hegemonic Culture: An Urgent Need for Marxist Reading Groups. *Radical Notes*. https://radicalnotes.org/2011/11/27/significance-of-a-counter-hegemonic-culture-an-urgent-need-for-marxist-reading-groups/.

____. 2012a. Why Must Social Science be Critical, and Why Must Doing Social Science be Difficult? *Radical Notes*. https://radicalnotes.

com/2012/11/03/why-must-social-science-be-critical-and-why-must-doing-social-science-be-difficult/.

____. 2012b. Thinking/Writing Theoretically About Society. *Radical Notes*. https://radicalnotes.org/2012/12/25/thinkingwriting-theoretically-about-society/.

____. 2012c. The Dirty Picture of Neoliberalism: India's New Economic Policy. *International Journal of Socialist Renewal*. http://links.org.au/node/2818.

____. 2012d. Forms of Subsumption of Labour Under Capital, Class Struggle and Uneven Development. *Review of Radical Political Economics* 44, No. 2: 178-200.

____. 2014a. *A Contribution to the Critique of Contemporary Capitalism: Theoretical and International Perspectives*. New York: Nova Science Publishers.

____. 2014b. Low-Wage Capitalism, Social Difference, and Nature-Dependent Production: A Study of the Conditions of Workers in Shrimp Aquaculture. *Human Geography: A New Radical Journal* 7, No. 1: 17-34.

____. 2014c. India in Crisis. *Canadian Dimension* 48, No. 2.

____. 2015. Critical Observations on Neo-liberalism and India's New Economic Policy. *Journal of Contemporary Asia* 45, No. 4: 715-726.

____. 2017a. *Marxist Class Theory for a Skeptical World*, Leiden/Boston: Brill.

____. 2017b. Social Movements and State Repression in India. *Journal of Asian and African Studies* 52, No. 8.

____. 2017c. David Harvey's Theory of Accumulation by Dispossession: A Marxist Critique. *World Review of Political Economy* 8, No. 4: 590-616.

____. 2020. *Critical Reflections on Economy and Politics in India: A Class Theory Perspective*. Leiden/Boston: Brill.

Dhillon, A. 2011. Reality Check for India's Economic Miracle. *Toronto Star*. https://www.thestar.com/opinion/editorialopinion/2011/09/03/reality_check_for_indias_e conomic_miracle.html.

Dreze, J. 2014. 'The Gujarat Muddle.' *The Hindu*. http://www.thehindu.com/opinion/op-ed/the-gujarat-muddle/article5896998.ece.

Dumenil, G. and Levy, D. 2005. The Neoliberal (Counter-) Revolution. In *Neoliberalism: A Critical Reader*, eds. A. Saad-Filho and D. Johnston. London: Pluto Press.

Eagleton, T. 1991. *Ideology*, London: Verso.

GOI (Government of India). 2007. *India: Rural Development Statistics: 2006-2007*. Hyderabad: National Institute of Rural Development.

Gunadasa, S. 2010. Fuelprice Hike Hits India's Poor. WSWS. http://www.wsws.org/en/articles/2010/06/indi-j30.html.

Harvey, D. 2003. *New Imperialism*. Oxford: Oxford University Press.

____. 2010. The Secret of Primitive Accumulation. In His *Companion to Marx's Capital*, 289–313. London: Verso.

Hasan, Z. 2014. Development and Doublespeak. *The Hindu*. http://www.thehindu.com/opinion/lead/development-and-doublespeak/article5897052.ece.

Hensman, R. 2014. The Gujarat Model of Development: What Would it Do to the Indian Economy? *Economic and Political Weekly*, Vol. XLIX, No. 11.

Herring, R. 1983. *The Political Economy of Agrarian Reform in South Asia*. Cornell: Cornell University Press.

Herring, R. and Agarwala, R. 2006. Restoring Agency to Class: Puzzles from the Subcontinent. *Critical Asian Studies* 38, No. 4: 323-356.

Khatkhate, D. 2006. Indian Economic Reform A Philosopher's Stone. *Economic and Political Weekly* 41, No. 22: 2203-2205.

Khera, R. 2008. Empowerment Guarantee Act. *Economic and Political Weekly* 43, No. 35: 8-10.

Kohli, A. 2012. *Poverty Amid Plenty in the New India*. Delhi: Cambridge University Press.

Kumar, A. 1999. Massacres by Landlord Militia Rock India's Second Most Populous State. WSWS. http://www.wsws.org/articles/1999/feb1999/ind2-f24.shtml

Laibman, D. 2016. *Passion and Patience: Society, History and Revolutionary Vision*. New York: International Publishers.

Lenin, V. 1961. *What is To Be Done*, https://www.marxists.org/archive/lenin/works/1901/witbd/.

Liberation. 2008. CAG Audit Interim Report: NREGA Being Mocked in Spirit? http://www.cpiml.org/liberation/year_2008/ February/cag_nrega.html.

Marx, K. 1976. *Wage-Labour and Capital*. New York: International Publishers.

____. 1977. *Capital*, Vol 1. New York: Vintage.

____. 1843. A Contribution to the Critique of Hegel's Philosophy of Right: Introduction https://www.marxists.org/archive/marx/works/1843/critique-hpr/intro.htm.

____. 1844. The Power of Money. In *Economic and Philosophic Manuscripts of 1844*, https://www.marxists.org/archive/marx/works/1844/manuscripts/power.htm.

____. 2000. *Selected Writings*, ed. by David McLellan. New York: Oxford University Press.

Marx, K. and Engels, F. 1982. *Selected Correspondence*. Moscow: Progress Publishers.

Misra, S. 2014. Farmers' Suicides in India, 1995-2012: Measurement and Interpretation. https://www.lse.ac.uk/asiaResearchCentre/_files/ARCWP62-Mishra.pdf.

Mohammad, N. 2017. Gujarat Isn't Doing Well on Bringing Down Its Infant Mortality Rate. *The Wire*. https://thewire.in/193304/gujarat-infant-mortality-rate.

Mukunthan, A. 2015. Rural India is Far Behind Urban India in Every Indicator of Progress, https://factly.in/rural-india-behind-urban-india-in-progress-indicators/.

Nanda, M. 2016. *Science in Saffron: Sceptical Essays on History of Science*. Gurgaon: Three Essays Collective.

Nandy, A. 2010. Ashis Nandy vs. the State of Gujarat: Authoritarian Developmentalism, Democracy and the Politics of Narendra Modi. *South Asian History and Culture* 1, No. 4: 577-596.

Patnaik, P. 1993. The Fascism of Our Times. *Social Scientist* 21, No. 3-4: 69-77.

____. ed. 2011. *Marx's Capital: An Introductory Reader*. New Delhi: Leftword Books.

Patnaik, U. 1986. The Agrarian Question and Development of Capitalism in India. *Economic and Political Weekly* 21, No. 18: 781-793.

____. 1990. *Agrarian Relations and Accumulation: The "Mode of Production Debate" in India*. Delhi: Oxford University Press.

____. 1999. *The Long Transition*. New Delhi: Tulika.

____. 2007. *The Republic of Hunger and Other Essays*. Gurgaon: Three Essays Collective.

Premchand. 1958. *Godaan: A Classic of Peasant India* (Translated by J. Ratan and P. Pal). Bombay: Jaico Books.

Pushpendra. 2000. Liberalization and Agrarian Reforms: Some Recent Controversies. In *Land Reforms in India*, eds. B.N. Sinha and Pushpendra, Vol. 5. pp. 45-63. New Delhi: Sage.

Rai, P. 2007. NREGA Battling Cancerous Corruption. India Together (available at: www.Indiatogether.org).

Riddell, J. 2011. The Origins of the United Front Policy. *International Socialism*, No. 130. http://isj.org.uk/the-origins-of-the-united-front-policy/.

Rudolph, L. and Rudolph, S. 1987. *In Pursuit of Lakshmi: The Political Economy of the Indian State*. Chicago: University of Chicago Press.

Sainath, P. 2009. Neo-Liberal Terrorism in India: The Largest Wave of Suicides in History. *Counterpunch*. http://www.counterpunch.org/sainath02122009.html.

____. 2013. Farmers' Suicide Rates Soar Above the Rest. *The Hindu*. http://www.thehindu.com/opinion/columns/sainath/farmers-suicide-rates-soar-above-the-rest/article4725101.ece.

____. 2014. Corporate Karza Maafi at Rs. 36.5 Trillion. Macroscan. http://www.macroscan.org/spfea/Jul14/pdf/Karza_Maafi.pdf.

Sayer, A. 1992. *Method in Social Science*. London: Routledge.

Sen, A. 1999. *Development as Freedom*. Oxford: Oxford University Press.

____. 2000. Freedom's Market. *The Guardian*. https://www.theguardian.com/world/2000/jun/25/globalisation.businessandmedia.

____. 2004. Sharing the World. http://www.littlemag.com/globalisation/amartyasen2.html.

____. 2005. *The Argumentative Indian*. London: Penguin.

Shariff, A. 1999. *India: Human Development Report*. New Delhi: Oxford University Press.

Shrimali, R. 2015. Spaces of Corporate Control in Agriculture: A Critical Study of Contract Farming in the Indian State of Punjab. (PhD dissertation). Toronto: York University.

Subramanian, S. 1998. Combating Naxalite Violence. http:// www.aapssindia.org/articles/ art2/naxalite.html.

Srinivasan, T. 2011. *Growth, Sustainability, and India's Economic Reforms*. Delhi: Oxford University Press.

Tagore, R. 2015 (1910). *Gitanjali*, New Delhi: FP Classics.

Thapar, R., Noorani, A. and Menon, S. 2016. *Nationalism*. New Delhi: Aleph Book Company.

*The Hindu* (2014). Country Can No Longer Wait for Reforms: Jaitley. *The Hindu*. http://www.thehindu.com/business/country-can-no-longer-wait-for-reforms-jaitley/article6722662.ece.

Trotsky, L. 1922. *The Question of the United Front*, https://www.marxists.org/archive/trotsky/1922/02/uf.htm.

____. 1931. For a Workers' United Front Against Fascism. https://www.marxists.org/archive/trotsky/germany/1931/311208.htm.

Wood, E. 1997. Back to Marx. *Monthly Review* 49, No. 2: 1-9.

Waghmare, A. 2017. Farmer Suicides Up 42 per cent in 2015, Second Consecutive Drought Year. http://www.indiaspend.com/cover-story/farmer-suicides-up-42-in-2015-second-consecutive-drought-year-43358.

Wittgenstein, L. 2001/1953. *Philosophical Investigations*. Oxford: Blackwell..

# Index

The fact that the electoral success of the formations such as AAP is seen as an alternative must be partly seen in the light of the failure of the Left, failure in ideological, political and organizational terms. The Left has failed to organize the masses on the basis of a socialist agenda. Indeed, sheer accommodation to the capitalist system characterizes the entire Left. It merely seeks to make the system a little more democratic, a little corruption free, a little more tolerable. It is this sort of ideological-political climate in which formations like AAP emerge.

2. This does not necessarily justify the support of the Left for a non-BJP government. An important question to ask is: while BJP was kept at bay, what was done to raise class consciousness of the masses and to mobilize them independently of bourgeois formations, in the sphere outside Parliament?

# 13

# Significance of a Counter-Hegemonic Left Culture

Capitalism creates poverty in various ways including by exploiting and over-exploiting workers, by making workers redundant through profit-seeking technical changes, and by dispossessing small-scale producers. Given that capitalism is an exploitative system, it prompts the masses to struggle against it, so capitalism requires poverty partly because poverty acts as a disciplining force on the masses. Capitalism causes and requires massive social and geographical inequality. And capitalism is inherently crisis-prone: capitalists collectively produce goods and services but cannot sell them all, so they cannot retrieve the money invested, which is when the system comes to a standstill. Workers remain un- and under-employed. Productive powers remain un- and under-used. We have just witnessed a major global economic crisis in 2008. In part because of its crisis-proneness, modern world capitalism is necessarily imperialist: advanced capitalist countries try to shift the effects of the crises they experience to politically and economically weaker countries (often with the connivance of the state in these countries). Normal mechanisms of capitalism and the combination of economic crisis and imperialism have major adverse impacts on the living conditions of the working masses in general and workers and poor peasants in the less developed countries such as India in particular.

No system of injustice goes unchallenged, however. Away from the preoccupations of the corporate-controlled mainstream